My Little Devos for Boys

365 Devotionals for Little Fellas

D0062585

Dayspring

LIVE YOUR FAITH

My Little Devo for Boys

Bible Translations Used:

HCSB: Scripture quotations marked HCSB® are taken from the Holman Christian Standard Bible®, Copyright © 1999, 2000, 2002, 2003, 2009 by Holman Bible Publishers. Used by permission. HCSB® is a federally registered trademark of Holman Bible Publishers.

NASB: Scripture quotations taken from the New American Standard Bible®, Copyright © 1960, 1962, 1963, 1968, 1971, 1972, 1973, 1975, 1977, 1995 by The Lockman Foundation Used by permission.

NCV: Scripture taken from the New Century Version. Copyright © 1987, 1988, 1991, 2005 by Thomas Nelson, Inc. Used by permission. All rights reserved.

NIV: Scripture quotations marked (NIV) are taken from the Holy Bible, New International Version®, NIV®. Copyright © 1973, 1978, 1984, 2011 by Biblica, Inc.™ Used by permission of Zondervan. All rights reserved worldwide. www.zondervan.com The "NIV" and "New International Version" are trademarks registered in the United States Patent and Trademark Office by Biblica, Inc.™

NKJV: Scripture taken from the New King James Version. Copyright © 1982 by Thomas Nelson, Inc. Used by permission. All rights reserved.

NLT: Holy Bible, New Living Translation, copyright © 1996, 2004, 2007, 2015 by Tyndale House Foundation. Used by permission of Tyndale House Publishers, Inc. All rights reserved.

Cover design by Kim Russell | wahoodesigns.com

ISBN: 978-1-68408-108-0

A Message to Parents

Congratulations on picking up this book of devotional readings for young boys. The fact that you're interested in this text proves that you're a thoughtful parent who understands the importance of teaching God's promises to your young child.

This book, which is intended to be read *by* Christian parents *to* their young children, is a collection of 365 chapters, one for each day of the year. If, during the next twelve months, you read a chapter each day, you'll enjoy 365 unique opportunities to share God's Word with your son, and that's a very good thing indeed.

God has given you a great opportunity and a profound responsibility: the opportunity to raise your child in a loving Christian home. If—even in some small way—the words on these pages can help you convey God's message to your youngster, this book will have served its purpose. So happy reading! And may the Lord bless you and your family now and forever.

‎✳ ✳ ✳

1
Start Your Day with God

*Morning by morning he wakens me
and opens my understanding to his will.
The Sovereign LORD has spoken to me, and I have listened.*

ISAIAH 50:4–5 NLT

How do you start your day? Do you snooze until the last possible minute and then hop out of bed without giving a single thought to God? Hopefully not. If you're smart, you'll start your day with a prayer of thanks to your heavenly Father.

Each new day is a gift from above, and if you're smart, you'll spend a few quiet moments thanking the Giver. It's the best way to start your day.

👉 Remember This

You need a regular appointment with your Father in heaven. God is ready to talk to you, and you should talk to Him every day.

✳ ✳ ✳

2
For God So Loved the World

For God so loved the world that He gave
His only begotten Son, that whoever believes in Him
should not perish but have everlasting life.

JOHN 3:16 NKJV

How much does God love you? He loves you so much that He sent His Son to die on the cross so that you might have an amazing blessing. That blessing is a gift called "eternal life," which means that you will live forever with God in heaven!

You don't have to be perfect to earn God's love. God simply wants you to put Jesus in your heart and keep Him there. So do yourself a favor right now: accept God's love with open arms and welcome Christ into your heart. When you do, your life will be changed today, tomorrow, and forever.

☞ Remember This

God loved the world so much that He sent His Son to die for our sins. His love is truly amazing!

✳ ✳ ✳

3
Share Your Faith

For in it God's righteousness is revealed from faith to faith,
just as it is written: The righteous will live by faith.

Are you genuinely excited about your faith? And do you show your enthusiasm to your friends and family? Hopefully so because God wants you to tell others about His Son.

Real Christianity is contagious. Excited Christians spread it around to friends, to neighbors, and even to complete strangers. So today and every day, share your faith and your excitement. The world needs both.

✳ ✳ ✳

Faith points us beyond our problems
to the hope we have in Christ.

BILLY GRAHAM

4

Choices That Make a Difference

Seek first God's kingdom and what God wants
Then all your other needs will be met as well.

MATTHEW 6:33 NCV

How do you make good choices? You can ask your parents, and they'll give you good advice. Or you can talk to your teachers, and they'll be glad to help you, too. But there's another source of wisdom that you can always use to help you figure things out. What is this source of wisdom that never fails? It's the Holy Bible.

Your choices are important. When you choose wisely, good things will usually happen. But if you make poor decisions, you can't expect to earn big rewards. So the next time you have an important decision to make, talk to your parents and talk to God. When you ask and listen, you'll make better choices, and you'll earn bigger rewards.

✳ ✳ ✳

The greatest choice any person makes
is to let God choose for him.

VANCE HAVNER

* * *

5
Good Thoughts

Finally brothers, whatever is true, whatever is honorable, whatever is just, whatever is pure, whatever is lovely, whatever is commendable—if there is any moral excellence and if there is any praise—dwell on these things.

PHILIPPIANS 4:8 HCSB

Do you try to think about things that are good, true, and helpful? The Bible says that you should. Do you try to pray several times each day? The Bible says that you should. Do you try to avoid bad thoughts and bad people? The Bible says that you should.

Your thoughts are powerful, and the Lord wants you to be careful. So, the Bible teaches you to guard your thoughts against things that are hurtful or wrong. When you avoid bad things and focus instead on Jesus, you will be protected and you will be blessed.

* * *

If you want to know whether you're thinking correctly, check it out in the Bible.

CHARLES STANLEY

✳ ✳ ✳

6
Trust God and Say Your Prayers

God answered their prayers because they trusted him.

1 Chronicles 5:20 MSG

Why do you pray? The answer, of course, is that you pray because you want to talk to God. But you shouldn't just talk to Him; you should also obey Him and trust Him.

When you trust the Lord's promises and obey His rules, you're on the right path. And when you decide to place God first in your life, you can be sure that He will bless you in surprising ways.

Your Father in heaven always keeps His promises. You can trust Him—and talk to Him—today, tomorrow, and forever.

✳ ✳ ✳

Prayer is talking with God. God knows your heart
and is not so concerned with your words
as He is with the attitude of your heart.

Josh McDowell

7
Share Your Blessings

Remember this: the person who sows sparingly
will also reap sparingly, and the person who
sows generously will also reap generously.

2 Corinthians 9:6 HCSB

God wants you to share the blessings He's given you, but it's not always easy to be generous. How many times have you heard someone say, "Don't touch that; it's mine!" If you're like most of us, you've heard those words many times and you may have even said them yourself.

The Bible teaches us that it's better to be generous than stingy. And the Bible also tells us that when we share, we'll be blessed.

So today and every day, do yourself—and other people—a favor: be a cheerful giver. It's the best way because it's God's way.

☞ Remember This

The more blessings you share, the more blessings you'll earn for yourself.

✳ ✳ ✳

8
Scattering Seeds of Kindness

Love each other like brothers and sisters. Give each other
more honor than you want for yourselves.

Romans 12:10 NCV

The Bible teaches us to love our neighbors. But we're so busy, and there's so little free time. So instead of helping our neighbors, we're tempted to ignore them.

This very day, you'll probably bump into somebody who needs a word of encouragement, or a pat on the back, or a helping hand, or a heartfelt prayer. And if you don't reach out to that person, who will?

Your Father in heaven wants you to be generous and kind. So today, look for a neighbor in need, and then do something to help. Father's orders.

☞ Remember This

You can never be sure when a kind word can change a person's day, or a person's life. So be quick to be kind.

✳ ✳ ✳

9

Make Every Day a Celebration

Always be full of joy in the Lord. I say it again—rejoice!

PHILIPPIANS 4:4 NLT

Do you feel like celebrating today? Are you expecting God to do wonderful things? Are you grateful for your family, your friends, your church, and your life? And do you appreciate the amazing gift of eternal life that is yours when you welcome Christ into your heart? Hopefully so, because the Lord has given you more blessings than you can possibly count. And He loves you now and forever, which means you have lots to celebrate.

This day, and every other day, is special. Treat it that way. And while you're celebrating, don't forget to say "thank You" to the Giver of all good gifts: your Father in heaven.

✳ ✳ ✳

Joy is the great note all throughout the Bible.

OSWALD CHAMBERS

✳ ✳ ✳
10
Finding Wisdom

*Understanding is like a fountain
which gives life to those who use it.*

PROVERBS 16:22 NCV

You've still lots to learn, and you're getting smarter every day. But it's not enough to learn things while you're at school. You should also study God's Word at home, you should listen carefully to your parents, and you should pay careful attention when you go to church.

To become wise, you must keep your eyes and ears open. You must learn to trust God's promises. And you must learn to obey the rules: your parents' rules *and* God's rules. When you do these things, there's no limit to the things you can learn.

☞ Remember This

The more you read your Bible, the wiser you'll be. Real wisdom begins with a willingness to trust God's Word.

✳ ✳ ✳

11
Courage for Today...and Forever

So don't worry, because I am with you. Don't be afraid,
because I am your God. I will make you strong and will help
you; I will support you with my right hand that saves you.

ISAIAH 41:10 NCV

When your own problems—or the world's problems—cause you to be afraid, you should discuss your fears with the people who love and care for you. Parents and grandparents can help you understand your fears, and they can help you feel better.

You should also pray about the things that worry you. God is always ready to hear your prayers, and He can give you comfort when you feel afraid. Whenever you're uncertain about what lies ahead, you can share your concerns with God...and you should.

☞ Remember This

If you're feeling worried or afraid, talk to your parents. And while you're at it, trust God to handle the problems that are simply too big for you or your family to solve.

12
Make Time for God

It is impossible to please God without faith.
Anyone who wants to come to him must believe that
God exists and that he rewards those who sincerely seek him.

HEBREWS 11:6 NLT

When it comes to spending time with God, are you a "squeezer" or a "pleaser"? Do you squeeze God into your schedule with a short prayer at bedtime, or do you please God by talking to Him far more often than that? If you're smart, you'll form the habit of spending lots of time with God every day.

Even if you're the busiest kid on earth, you can still make time for God. And when you think about it, isn't that the very least you should do?

 **A Timely Tip**

If you want to have a great life, spend time with God every day.

✳ ✳ ✳

13
Expecting Great Things

When a believing person prays, great things happen.

JAMES 5:16 NCV

The Bible teaches us that when believing Christians pray, great things can happen. When you pray, do you expect great things to happen? Do you expect God to do big things? You should. The Lord can work miracles of all sizes—big ones, little ones, and in-between ones—because nothing is too hard for Him.

God has big plans for you, and He will help you stay on the right path if you ask Him to. So ask Him…and when you do, expect great things to happen!

✳ ✳ ✳

We honor God by asking for great things
when they are a part of His promise. We dishonor Him
and cheat ourselves when we ask for molehills
where He has promised mountains.

VANCE HAVNER

14
Wasted Words

If anyone thinks he is religious without controlling his tongue, then his religion is worthless and he deceives himself.

JAMES 1:26 HCSB

When we talk about people behind their backs, it's called gossip. Gossip is a waste of time and a waste of words. No wonder the Bible teaches us that gossip is wrong.

The next time you're tempted to say an unkind word about somebody who's not around to defend himself—or herself—slow down and think before you speak. And if you can't think of something kind to say... keep thinking!

⌗ Remember This

It's always better to say nothing than to say something you wish you hadn't said.

✳ ✳ ✳

15
Love One Another

Above all, keep fervent in your love for one another,
because love covers a multitude of sins.

1 PETER 4:8 HCSB

Just like the song says, Jesus loves you. And He wants you to share His love with other people. Of course, some folks are easier to love than others. The people who are friendly, kind, and happy—they're easy to love. But what about the people who aren't so nice? Well, Jesus wants you to love them, too.

Christ wants you to love all people, not just the lovable ones. That means that you should forgive everybody as quickly as you can. And you should try hard to share Christ's love with everybody. No exceptions.

He who is filled with love is filled with God Himself.

ST. AUGUSTINE

* * *

16
Room to Grow

*Grow in grace and understanding of our Master and Savior,
Jesus Christ. Glory to the Master, now and forever! Yes!*

2 PETER 3:18 MSG

You still have room to grow. And that's good because
when it comes to your faith, God doesn't intend for you
to become "fully grown," at least not in this lifetime.

As a Christian, you should continue to grow in the
love and the knowledge of your Savior as long as you
live. How? By studying God's Word, by obeying His
commandments, and by allowing His Son to reign in
your heart.

* * *

*A Christian is never in a state of completion
but always in the process of becoming.*

MARTIN LUTHER

✳ ✳ ✳

17
God Knows Best

"I say this because I know what I am planning for you,"
says the LORD. "I have good plans for you,
not plans to hurt you. I will give you hope and a good future."

God has a plan for you. But the Lord's plan may not always work out exactly like you want it to. Still, God always knows best. Sometimes, even though you may want something very badly, you must be patient and wait for the right time to get it. So who, exactly, determines the right time? That's up to God. He's always in control.

If there's something you want very badly, ask for God's help, and keep asking. Trust Him always, obey Him always, and wait for Him to show you His plans. When the time is right, He will make things clear.

☞ Remember This

God has a wonderful plan for your life. When you obey His teachings and follow His Son, He'll help you make wise choices.

20

***

18
Shine Like a Star

The wise people will shine like the brightness of the sky.
Those who teach others to live right will shine like stars
forever and ever.

DANIEL 12:3 NCV

The Bible promises that if you show other people what it means to trust God and obey Him, you'll shine like a star forever. When you stop to think about it, that's an amazing promise.

God wants you to grow up to be a wise person. And your parents want the same thing. So keep reading, keep studying, keep praying, and keep learning how to behave like a Christian. When you do these things, you'll grow up to be a star, shining brightly forever.

☞ Remember This

If you pay attention to God's Word and live by it, you'll be a star!

✳ ✳ ✳

19
Share the Good News

*For God has not given us a spirit of fear and timidity,
but of power, love, and self-discipline.
So never be ashamed to tell others about our Lord.*

2 TIMOTHY 1:7–8 NLT

God wants us to talk about His Son. So every Christian, each in our own way, should spread the Good News about Jesus. But talking about our faith isn't enough. We shouldn't just sound like Christians; we should also behave like Christians.

Today and every day, be quick to tell people about Jesus. Don't be shy or afraid to talk about your faith. Think of it as "show and tell." First, you show people what it means to follow Christ; then you tell them about it.

✳ ✳ ✳

*The sermon of your life in tough times ministers to people
more powerfully than the most eloquent speaker.*

BILL BRIGHT

20
Eternal Life: God's Priceless Gift

I have written these things to you who believe
in the name of the Son of God, so that you may know
that you have eternal life.

1 JOHN 5:13 HCSB

Jesus gave up His life on the cross so that we might have eternal life. That gift, freely given from God's only begotten Son, is the priceless possession of everyone who accepts Him as Lord and Savior.

God is waiting patiently for each of us to accept the gift of eternal life. If you've already welcomed Jesus into your heart, then your place in heaven is secure. But if you're still trying to make up your mind, today is the perfect day to say "yes" to Jesus.

At most, you will live a hundred years on earth,
but you will spend forever in eternity.

RICK WARREN

✳ ✳ ✳

21
Be a Disciple

"Follow Me," He told them, "and I will make you fish for people!" Immediately they left their nets and followed Him.

MATTHEW 4:19–20 HCSB

The Bible promises that when you follow in Christ's footsteps, you will learn how to behave yourself, and you'll learn how to live a very good life. Jesus wants you to become a new person through Him. And that's exactly what you should want for yourself, too. So talk with Jesus (through prayer) and walk with Him (by obeying His rules) today and forever.

Who will you walk with today? Do yourself a favor—walk with Jesus!

✳ ✳ ✳

God's purpose is that we be disciples and then make disciples.

CHARLES STANLEY

22
Expecting God's Blessings

My cup runs over. Surely goodness and mercy shall follow me all the days of my life; and I will dwell in the house of the LORD forever.

PSALM 23:5–6 NKJV

Do you expect God to keep His promises and bless you today, tomorrow, and forever? You should. God always keeps His promises, and He has very big plans for you. That's why you should be an optimistic Christian, always praising God for His gifts.

When you think about it, you've got more blessings than you can count. So make it a habit to thank God for the gifts He's given you, and don't waste time worrying about the things you don't have. When you praise the Lord and follow in the footsteps of His Son, more blessings are sure to be arriving soon.

✳ ✳ ✳

*Keep your feet on the ground,
but let your heart soar as high as it will.*

A. W. TOZER

23
Everybody Makes Mistakes

The LORD says, "Forget what happened before,
and do not think about the past. Look at the new thing
I am going to do. It is already happening. Don't you see it?
I will make a road in the desert and rivers in the dry land."

ISAIAH 43:18–19 NCV

Nobody likes to make mistakes, but everybody makes them. And you're no different! When you make mistakes (and you will), you should correct them, you should learn from them, and you should avoid making the same mistake twice.

If you want to become smarter faster, you'll learn from your mistakes the first time. And that's good because the biggest mistake you can make is to keep making the same mistake over and over and over again.

Father, take our mistakes and turn them into opportunities.

MAX LUCADO

✳✳✳

24
Keep Learning and Growing

*When I was a child, I spoke and thought
and reasoned as a child.
But when I grew up, I put away childish things.*

1 CORINTHIANS 13:11 NLT

When will you be fully grown up? Hopefully never! God wants you continue to grow as a Christian throughout your entire life.

If you try, you can grow closer to the Lord day by day, and that's good because He has many wonderful lessons He wants to teach you. When you learn from His Word and talk to Him through your prayers, God will show you ways to become a better person and a better Christian. So, keep learning from your heavenly Father. And never stop.

God's goal is that we move toward maturity.

CHARLES SWINDOLL

✳ ✳ ✳

25
Be a Humble Servant

The great among you must be a servant.
But those who exalt themselves will be humbled,
and those who humble themselves will be exalted.

MATTHEW 23:11–12 NLT

Who are the greatest people in God's eyes? Are they the richest, the most famous, and the most powerful people in the world? Nope. The greatest people you'll ever meet are the humble servants who care less about themselves and more about following Jesus.

When something good happens to you, it's tempting to take all the credit. So you may be tempted to say, "Look at me! I did that!" But nothing could be further from the truth. All of your blessings come from God, and He deserves the credit. So when something good happens, be humble, be grateful, and give praise to the proper source: God.

👉 Remember This

Jesus had a humble heart. And if we want to follow in His footsteps, we must be humble, too.

26
Good Behavior Is Wise Behavior

A foolish person enjoys doing wrong, but a person
with understanding enjoys doing what is wise.

PROVERBS 10:23 NCV

Some people might try to convince you that it's fun to misbehave, but they're wrong. No matter what other people say, it's always better to do the right thing...and it's more fun, too.

When you do something that you know is wrong, your conscience—that little voice in your head that tells you right from wrong—makes you feel worried, sorry, and afraid. You're worried about what you did; you're sorry that you did it; and you're afraid that you'll get caught.

So, the next time somebody encourages you to misbehave, say no loudly and clearly. It's the right thing to do, and it's the only way to have a clear conscience.

✳✳✳

The more wisdom enters our hearts, the more we will
be able to trust our hearts in difficult situations.

JOHN ELDREDGE

✳ ✳ ✳

27
God Has Big Plans for You

But as it is written in the Scriptures: "No one has ever seen this, and no one has ever heard about it. No one has ever imagined what God has prepared for those who love him."

1 Corinthians 2:9 NCV

God has plans for you. Very big plans. He put you here for a reason: His reason. And He knows precisely where He wants you to go and how He wants you to get there.

Of course, you've still got lots of growing up to do, and you've still got lots to learn. But while you're trying to figure things out—and while you're trying to understand God's plan for you—please remember this: God wants to guide you to a place that He has chosen especially for you. Your job is to listen, to learn, and to follow wherever the Lord leads.

☞ Remember This

Since God is your protector, aim high. You and God, working together, can do big things.

✳ ✳ ✳

28
Good Thoughts and Good Deeds

They are blessed whose thoughts are pure,
for they will see God.

MATTHEW 5:8 NCV

God wants you to think good thoughts and do good deeds, but if you're sad or tired, you may not feel like it. That's when the Lord wants you to slow down, rest up, and think about what His love means to you.

God has been very good to you. He's given you more blessings than you can count. Now, He wants you to share some of those blessings, and He wants you to be grateful.

So, today and every day, try to think good thoughts and do nice things for people who need your help. When you do, you'll be happier; you'll make other people happier; and you'll make God happy, too.

✳ ✳ ✳

It is the thoughts and intents of the heart
that shape a person's life.

JOHN ELDREDGE

29
Hard Work Pays Off

A lazy person will end up poor,
but a hard worker will become rich.

PROVERBS 10:4 NCV

Have you figured out that it's always best to do first things first? Or are you one of those boys who puts important things off until the last minute?

God's Word teaches us that it's always best to do our work first and save our playtime for later. But with so many fun things to occupy our minds and gobble up our time, we're tempted to choose fun and games first. We tell ourselves that we'll get around to the important stuff later, but sometimes "later" really means "never."

You have an opportunity to do great things for God, but you'll have to work at it. So pray as if everything depended upon God, and work as if everything depended upon you. When you do, you'll be surprised at the amazing things that you and the Lord, working together, can do.

* * *

Success or failure can be pretty well predicted
by the degree to which the heart is fully in it.

JOHN ELDREDGE

30

God Loves You Now and Forever!

Praise him, all you people of the earth.
For his unfailing love for us is powerful;
the LORD's faithfulness endures forever. Praise the LORD!

PSALM 117:1–2 NLT

Where can we find God's love? Everywhere. His love reaches beyond the heavens, and it touches the smallest corner of every human heart. His love does not arrive someday—it arrives instantly and it never ends.

God loves this world so much that He sent His Son to save it. And now, God wants you to put Jesus first in your life. When you do, you'll be very, very glad. Why? Because you'll experience God's love now and forever.

☞ Remember This

God's love for you doesn't come and go. He's always with you, always ready to hear your prayers and help you make wise choices.

Understanding Christ's Love

*And I pray that you and all God's holy people will have the power
to understand the greatness of Christ's love—how wide and how
long and how high and how deep that love is. Christ's love is greater
than anyone can ever know, but I pray that you will be able to know
that love. Then you can be filled with the fullness of God.*

EPHESIANS 3:18–19 NCV

The Bible says that Jesus loves you. It's an amazing promise with a very happy ending: Christ has already prepared a place for you in heaven. So how should this Good News make you feel? The fact that Jesus loves you should make you a very happy boy, so happy, in fact, that you try your best to do the things that please Him.

Jesus wants you to love and obey God, and He wants you to be kind to everybody. These are simple instructions from the Son of God. Please take them seriously.

✳ ✳ ✳

*Christ is like a river that is continually flowing. There are always
fresh supplies of water coming from the fountain-head, so that a
man may live by it and be supplied with water all his life. They who
live upon Christ may have fresh supplies from him for all eternity.*

JONATHAN EDWARDS

✳ ✳ ✳

32

Time Is Valuable; Don't Waste It!

A hard worker has plenty of food,
but a person who chases fantasies has no sense.

PROVERBS 12:11 NLT

Today, it's easier than ever to waste time. There are so many amazing shows, so many amazing games, and so many amazing toys that can gobble up hours at a time. So how much time is left for more important things, like doing your homework or reading your Bible? Not much time at all.

Of course you should have fun. But you shouldn't let fun and games eat up *all* your time. Schoolwork is important. And God wants you to spend time with Him, too.

So, if you're in the habit of doing fun stuff first and important stuff later (or not at all), it's time for a change. Do the important things first, and you'll still have plenty of time for the fun stuff after you're finished.

☞ Remember This

When God gives you an important job, He'll also give you enough time to finish it.

33

Be Enthusiastic!

I tell you the truth, whoever believes in me will do the same things that I do. Those who believe will do even greater things than these, because I am going to the Father.

JOHN 14:12 NCV

Are you enthusiastic about your life, your friends, your faith, and your future? Are you quick to celebrate the victories of others, and are you determined to do what you can to make the world a happier place? Hopefully so! After all, just about everybody you happen to meet needs your encouragement and your enthusiasm. And you deserve the joy of sharing it.

Genuine enthusiasm is contagious; other people can catch it from you. So if you're at home, school, church, or just about anywhere else, be enthusiastic. Your friends and family need to hear from a cheerful person…like you!

✳ ✳ ✳

One of the great needs in the church today is for every Christian to become enthusiastic about his faith in Jesus Christ.

BILLY GRAHAM

***

34

Don't Blame Other People

When they continued to ask Jesus their question,
he raised up and said, "Anyone here who
has never sinned can throw the first stone at her."

JOHN 8:7 NCV

When something goes wrong, do you look for somebody to blame? And if you make a mistake, do you try to make it look like somebody else did it? Hopefully not! It's dishonest—and unkind—to blame other people for your own problems, so don't do it.

If you've done something wrong, don't look for somebody to blame; look for a way to fix the problem you've created. Then say, "I'm sorry, and I won't make that same mistake again." When you admit your mistakes, you can learn from them. And that's exactly what you should do.

 **A Timely Tip**

Since you can't really win the blame game, it isn't smart to play.

***

35
White Lies?

Doing right brings freedom to honest people.

PROVERBS 11:6 NCV

People sometimes convince themselves that it's okay to tell "little white lies." They tell themselves that small lies aren't harmful. But there's a problem: little lies have a way of growing into big ones, and once they grow up, they can cause lots of problems.

Remember that lies, no matter what size, can be harmful to your spiritual health. So tell the truth about everything. It's the right thing to do, and it's the best way to live.

***

Those who are given to white lies soon become color-blind.

ANONYMOUS

* * *
36
Some Days Are Hard

We take the good days from God—why not also the bad days?

JOB 2:10 MSG

Some days are harder than others. Sometimes you may feel angry or sad, but you may not understand why you feel that way. Maybe you're tired, or disappointed, or afraid. Or maybe you just got up on the wrong side of the bed!

God has lots of good things in store for you, but until you start thinking good thoughts, you won't be in the right kind of mood to accept all of His gifts.

On those days when you're feeling out of sorts, it's time to calm down, it's time to rest up, it's time to collect your thoughts, and it's time to count your blessings—and it's time to keep counting those blessings until you feel better.

 A Timely Tip

When you have a problem, don't get discouraged. Just do your best to solve the problem and leave the rest up to the Lord.

*** *** ***

37
What Would Jesus Say?

A good person produces good deeds
and words season after season.

MATTHEW 12:35 MSG

Do you like for people to say kind things to you? Of course you do! And that's exactly how other people feel, too. That's why it's so important to say things that make people feel better, not worse.

If you're not sure what to say, ask yourself what Jesus might say if He were standing by your side. Jesus always said helpful things, not hurtful things. You can, too.

You'll feel better about yourself when you help other people feel better about themselves, so choose your words wisely. Everybody needs to hear kind words, and that's exactly the kind of words they should hear from you!

 A Timely Tip

If you're not sure what to say, ask yourself this question: "What would Jesus say if He were here?" Then you'll have the answer.

38
Church Can Be Fun!

The church, you see, is not peripheral to the world;
the world is peripheral to the church. The church
is Christ's body, in which he speaks and acts,
by which he fills everything with his presence.

EPHESIANS 1:23 MSG

When your parents take you to church, are you pleased? Hopefully so. After all, church is a great place to learn about God's rules and God's Son.

The church belongs to the Lord just as surely as you belong to Him. So when your parents take you to church, don't be sad, gloomy, or bored; be happy. Your church is a fine, fun place to be...and you're fortunate to be there.

Remember This

Your attitude about church makes a big difference. So when you go to church, keep a positive attitude.

✳ ✳ ✳

39
No Problems Are Too Big for God

For the LORD your God is the God of gods and Lord of lords,
the great, mighty, and awesome God.

DEUTERONOMY 10:17 HCSB

*A*re you worried about a problem that you haven't been able to solve? Welcome to the club! Life is full of problems that don't have easy solutions.

The Lord has a way of helping us solve our problems if we let Him; our job is to let Him. And the sooner we turn our concerns over to Him, the sooner He will begin fixing the things that are simply too big for us to handle.

If you're worried or discouraged, pray about it. And ask your parents and friends to pray about it, too. Then, stop worrying because no problem is too big for God; not even yours.

✳ ✳ ✳

The next time you're disappointed, don't panic. Don't give up.
Just be patient and let God remind you He's still in control.

MAX LUCADO

* * *

40
Be Quick to Be Kind

Kind people do themselves a favor,
but cruel people bring trouble on themselves.

PROVERBS 11:17 NCV

The Bible promises that if you're a kind person, good things will happen to you. That's one reason (but not the only reason) that it's important to be kind.

Do you listen to your heart when it tells you to be nice to other people? Hopefully, you do. After all, lots of people in the world aren't as fortunate as you are. So ask your parents to help you find ways to do nice things for people who need your help. And don't forget that everybody needs love, kindness, and respect, so you should always be ready to share those things, too.

* * *

If we have the true love of God in our hearts, we will show
it in our lives. We will not have to go up and down the earth
proclaiming it. We will show it in everything we say or do.

D. L. MOODY

41
Obey and Be Happy

Praise the LORD! Happy are those who respect the LORD,
who want what he commands.

PSALM 112:1 NCV

Do you want to be happy? Then you should learn to obey your parents and your teachers. And you should also learn to obey God. When you do, you'll discover that happiness goes hand in hand with good behavior.

The happiest people do not misbehave; the happiest people are not greedy or mean. The happiest people don't disobey their parents, their teachers, or their Father in heaven. The happiest people are the ones who obey the rules. Make sure you're one of those people.

＊＊＊

True faith commits us to obedience.

A. W. TOZER

✳︎ ✳︎ ✳︎

42
Use Your Talents

Now there are different gifts, but the same Spirit.
There are different ministries, but the same Lord.

1 Corinthians 12:4–5 HCSB

God has been very good to you. He's given you very special talents, talents that you can use to make the world a better place. So here's a question: will you use your talents or not? God wants you to use your talents to become a better person and a better Christian. And you should want that, too.

As you're trying to figure out exactly what you're good at, pray about it. And be sure to talk things over with your parents. They can help you decide how best to use and improve the gifts God has given you. And remember this: a great way to thank God for your gifts is to use them.

✳︎ ✳︎ ✳︎

You aren't an accident. You were deliberately planned,
specifically gifted, and lovingly positioned
on this earth by the Master Craftsman.

Max Lucado

✳ ✳ ✳

43
The Power of Hope

Let all that I am wait quietly before God,
for my hope is in him.

PSALM 62:5 NLT

If you trust God's promises, you should never lose hope. After all, the Bible teaches us that God is good and that His love endures forever. But even though you know these things, you may get discouraged from time to time. That's when you should remember that God is faithful and you're protected.

So the next time you have a difficult problem, pray as if everything depended on God, work as if everything depended on you, and never lose hope. God will never give up on you; please don't ever give up on Him.

☞ Remember This

Because the Lord is on your side—and by your side—you should never lose hope. With God, all things are possible.

✳✳✳
44
Growing Up Day by Day

As newborn babies want milk, you should want the pure and simple teaching. By it you can mature in your salvation.

1 PETER 2:2 NCV

You're growing up day by day. Every day you're learning new things and doing new things. And there's no need to stop.

Do you think it's smart to keep growing and growing and growing? If you said "yes," you're right. So remember: you're a very special person today...and you'll be just as special when you've grown a little bit more tomorrow.

☞ Remember This

God has many things He wants to teach you. And you can learn important things at home, at church, and at school. If you keep your eyes and ears open, you can learn new things every day...and you should.

✳ ✳ ✳

45

Your Relationship with Jesus

*I am the Vine, you are the branches. When you're joined
with me and I with you, the relation intimate and organic,
the harvest is sure to be abundant.*

John 15:5 MSG

What kind of relationship do you have with Jesus? Is He your very best friend, or do you hardly know Him? Hopefully, you're getting to know Jesus very well.

When you invite Christ into your heart, He will be your friend forever.

If you make mistakes, Jesus will still be your friend. If you behave badly, He will still love you. If you feel sorry or sad, Christ can help you feel better.

Jesus wants you to have a happy, healthy life. He wants you to follow Him; He wants you to behave yourself; and He wants you to take care of yourself. Why? Because He loves you, today, tomorrow, and forever. That's the kind of relationship He wants with you.

 **A Timely Tip**

God has a better plan. He wants you to look before you leap. Why? Because if you leap before you look, you may land in a very bad place.

✳ ✳ ✳

46

It's Important to Forgive

Sensible people control their temper;
they earn respect by overlooking wrongs.

PROVERBS 19:11 NLT

The Bible teaches us that we should forgive the people who have hurt us. But sometimes, it's hard to forgive and forget. Very hard.

If you're unwilling to forgive someone, you're building a roadblock between yourself and God. And you're creating a problem for yourself that you certainly don't need.

So if you really want to forgive someone, pray for that person. And then pray for yourself by asking God to help you forgive. Don't expect forgiveness to be easy or quick, but with God as your helper, you can forgive . . . and you will.

 A Timely Tip

If you want to obey God's rules, you must forgive other people. It's not optional. If you refuse to forgive, you're disobeying the Lord. So be quick to forgive everybody.

47
Who Are You Trying to Please?

Do not be deceived: "Bad company corrupts good morals."

1 CORINTHIANS 15:33 HCSB

Sooner or later it happens to everybody: a friend asks us to do something that we think is wrong. What should we do? Should we try to please our friend while making a poor choice? Absolutely not. It's not worth it! Trying to please our friends is okay. What's not okay is misbehaving in order to please them.

Do you have a friend who encourages you to misbehave? Hopefully you don't have any friends like that. But if you do, please be ready to say, "No way!" And what if your friend threatens to break up the friendship? Let him! Friendships like that aren't worth the trouble.

✳ ✳ ✳

Do you want to be wise? Choose wise friends.

CHARLES SWINDOLL

* * *

48
You Can Do It

I am able to do all things through Him who strengthens me.

PHILIPPIANS 4:13 HCSB

Do you have big plans and big dreams? And do you believe that with God's help you can achieve those dreams? If you answered yes to both questions, you're on the right track.

Nothing is too difficult for the Lord, and no dreams are too big for Him—not even yours. So keep dreaming, and keep doing the work that's required to make your dreams come true. You and God, working together, can do amazing things.

☞ Remember This

If you have a big dream, don't be afraid to go for it. You and God, working together, can do big things.

✳ ✳ ✳

49
God Has the Final Say

People may make plans in their minds,
but the LORD decides what they will do.

PROVERBS 16:9 NCV

If God is good, and if He controls everything, why do bad things happen? Part of that question is easy to answer: Sometimes bad things happen because people choose to disobey God's rules. When they break the rules—especially God's rules—they create trouble. It's unfortunate but it happens. But on other occasions, bad things happen, and it's nobody's fault. Sometimes things just happen and we simply cannot know why. Thankfully, the Bible teaches us that all our questions will be answered someday. When we finally get to heaven, we will understand all the reasons behind God's plans. But until then, we must simply trust the Lord and depend upon Him, knowing that He always keeps His promises.

✳ ✳ ✳

Rest in God's goodness, believing that
He has all things under His control.

CHARLES SWINDOLL

***

50
Don't Fight!

*Foolish people lose their tempers,
but wise people control theirs.*

PROVERBS 29:11 NCV

Since the days of Cain and Abel—two men who were sons of Adam and Eve—people have discovered plenty of things to fight about. It seems that fighting is a favorite activity for many people, even though it's almost always the wrong thing to do.

If you're familiar with the Bible, you already know that Christians should do their best to avoid fights. Whether you're six, or sixty, or a hundred and six, it's better to live peacefully than angrily. So do yourself a favor: try to avoid senseless scuffles, foolish fights, alarming arguments, and constant conflicts. You'll be glad you did . . . and so will God.

 **A Timely Tip**

If you're faced with a hard choice, ask yourself what Jesus would do. The answer will tell you which choice is best.

51
Following His Footsteps

But whoever keeps His word, truly in him the love of God is perfected. This is how we know we are in Him: the one who says he remains in Him should walk just as He walked.

1 JOHN 2:5–6 HCSB

Jesus walks with you. Are you walking with Him? Hopefully you will choose to walk with Him today and every day of your life.

Jesus has called upon believers of every generation (and that includes you) to follow in His footsteps. Will you follow Him? Hopefully you will. When you welcome Jesus into your heart, you'll always be glad you did. Always!

☞ **Remember This**

When you're following in Christ's footsteps, you can be sure that you're on the right path.

* * *

52
Aim High

I can do all things through Christ,
because he gives me strength.

PHILIPPIANS 4:13 NCV

God has big plans for you. Very big plans. He put you here for a reason, and He has important things He wants you to accomplish. The Lord believes in you…do you believe in yourself? You should.

The Bible teaches us that we can do amazing things when we depend on God. So don't be afraid to aim high. You and God, working together, can do things that would be impossible for you to do by yourself.

* * *

You cannot out-dream God.

JOHN ELDREDGE

*** *** ***

53
It Pays to Work Hard

*A person who doesn't work hard
is just like someone who destroys things.*

PROVERBS 18:9 NCV

God wants you to obey Him now, not later. And He wants you to do what needs to be done when it needs to be done. Not later.

Have you formed the habit of putting things off? If so, today is a perfect day to make a new habit: the habit of doing the most important jobs first.

God has big plans for you, but He won't force you to do the work that's needed to make those plans come true. He'll do His part, but He expects you to do your part, too.

Doing the Lord's work is a responsibility that you should take seriously. When you do, your loving heavenly Father gladly gives you the rewards you've earned.

*** *** ***

*Let us not be content to wait and see what will happen,
but give us the determination to make the right things happen.*

PETER MARSHALL

✳ ✳ ✳
54
Trust God's Truth

You will know the truth, and the truth will set you free.

John 8:32 HCSB

Jesus had a message for His followers and for you. He said, "The truth will set you free."

When we tell the truth, we don't need to worry about our lies catching up with us. And when we behave honestly, we don't have to worry about feeling guilty or ashamed. But if we fail to do what we know is right, we make trouble for ourselves, and we feel guilty for the things we've done.

Jesus understood that the truth is a very good thing indeed. You should understand it, too.

☞ Remember This

When you trust God's truth and live by it, you'll be blessed, and you'll be protected...now and forever.

55
Encouraging Words for Your Family

Good people's words will help many others.

PROVERBS 10:21 NCV

Life can be hard sometimes. So every member of your family—including you—needs encouragement.

In the book of Ephesians, Paul writes, "When you talk, do not say harmful things, but say what people need—words that will help others become stronger. Then what you say will do good to those who listen to you" (4:29 NCV). Paul reminds us that when we choose our words carefully, we can help the people we love.

Today, be sure to tell your family members how much you love and appreciate them. When you do, you'll make everybody happy.

* * *

We have the Lord, but he Himself has recognized that we need the touch of a human hand. He Himself came down and lived among us as a man. We cannot see Him now, but blessed be the tie that binds human hearts in Christian love.

VANCE HAVNER

*** ***

56
When People Are Cruel

A kind man benefits himself,
but a cruel man brings disaster on himself.

PROVERBS 11:17 HCSB

If all the people in the world could just be kind to each other, this world would be a much better place. But it doesn't work that way. Sometimes people can be cruel, and occasionally they can be very cruel.

When other people are unkind to you or to your friends, you may be tempted to strike back in anger. Don't do it! Instead, remember that God corrects other people's behaviors in His own way, and He doesn't need your help.

When people misbehave, try to be patient and try to be kind. Remember that God wants you to forgive everybody, even when it's hard. So forgive and move on as quickly as you can. And leave the rest up to God.

☞ Remember This

When other kids are being unkind, don't join in. God wants you to treat everybody with respect, even when others don't.

57
Keep Your Eyes on Jesus

Let us fix our eyes on Jesus, the author and perfecter of our faith, who for the joy set before him endured the cross, scorning its shame, and sat down at the right hand of the throne of God.

HEBREWS 12:2 NIV

Today and every day, keep your eyes on Jesus. Do your best to follow Him and honor Him with your words, with your prayers, and with your actions.

Jesus came into this world so that you might have a good life and (more importantly) eternal life. So, welcome Him into your heart and invite Him to rule over your life.

Christ wants you to follow His example. You can learn about the things He did, and you can try hard to be like Him. Jesus was a kind and loving servant. And He trusted His Father in heaven. You can be kind, and generous, and trusting, too. And that's what Christ wants you to do.

✳ ✳ ✳

You must never sacrifice your relationship with God for the sake of a relationship with another person.

CHARLES STANLEY

58
It's Important to Make Good Choices

Merely hearing God's law is a waste of your time
if you don't do what he commands. Doing, not hearing,
is what makes the difference with God.

ROMANS 2:13 MSG

The things you choose to say and do can make a big difference in your life. If you make good choices, good things will usually happen to you. But if you make poor choices, bad things can happen, and fast.

The next time you have an important choice to make, ask yourself this: "Am I doing what God wants me to do?" If the answer to that question is "Yes," go ahead. But if you're not sure, slow down, think things over, and say a prayer. Why? Because the decisions you make today can make a big difference in your life tomorrow. Good decisions bring big rewards; poor decisions don't. So choose carefully.

* * *

There are two masters, and you have to choose
which master you are going to serve.

BILLY GRAHAM

59
Silly Arguments Aren't Worth It

But stay away from those who have foolish arguments
and talk about useless family histories and argue
and quarrel about the law. Those things are
worth nothing and will not help anyone.

TITUS 3:9 NCV

Silly arguments always cause more problems than they solve. And God's Word makes it clear that foolish arguments should be avoided. So the next time you're tempted to argue with somebody, avoid the temptation. Instead of losing your temper, stay calm. And remember that you don't have to attend every argument you're invited to.

∗ ∗ ∗

Some fights are lost even though we win.
A bulldog can whip a skunk, but it just isn't worth it.

VANCE HAVNER

60
When You Do the Right Thing

His master replied, "Well done, good and faithful servant!
You have been faithful with a few things;
I will put you in charge of many things.
Come and share your master's happiness!"

MATTHEW 25:21 NIV

God loves you, and He wants you to follow in the footsteps of His Son. The Lord wants you to read His Word and follow His instructions. In other words, God wants you to do the right thing today and every day.

When you obey God, you'll be blessed. So try hard, do your best, and honor your Father in heaven. When you do, God will help you and guide you. And you'll be amazed at the things you can do when the Lord lends a helping hand.

✳ ✳ ✳

If you seek to know the path of your duty,
use God as your compass.

C. H. SPURGEON

* * *

61
Amazing Grace

Let us, then, feel very sure that we can come before God's throne where there is grace. There we can receive mercy and grace to help us when we need it.

HEBREWS 4:16 NCV

God's grace is a gift you didn't earn—in fact, you can never earn it. No matter how hard you might try, you can never be perfect enough to deserve the priceless gift of eternal life. Thankfully, God knows that you're not perfect, and He loves you anyway. He loves you so much, in fact, that He sent His Son to die for you, and for every other person who accepts Jesus.

Now, you have another chance to thank the Lord for blessings that are simply too numerous to count. Today is a wonderful day to thank God for His love, for His Son, and for His grace.

☞ Remember This

You don't have to earn God's love. He gives it for free. Your job is simple: accept it.

* * *

62
Encourage Each Other

So encourage each other and give each other strength,
just as you are doing now.

1 Thessalonians 5:11 NCV

When other people are sad, we can do our best to cheer them up by showing kindness and love.

The Bible teaches us that we must care for each other, and when everybody is happy, that's an easy thing to do. But when people are sad or afraid, it's up to us to say a kind word or to offer a helping hand.

Do you know someone who is discouraged or sad? If so, think of something you can do to cheer that person up …and then do it. You'll make two people happy.

* * *

The Bible teaches us to be more concerned about the needs
and feelings of others than our own. We are to encourage
our loved ones, friends, and associates.

Billy Graham

63

It Pays to Behave

Dear friend, do not imitate what is evil,
but what is good. The one who does good is of God;
the one who does evil has not seen God.

3 JOHN 1:11 HCSB

Do you behave differently because you're a Christian? Are you nicer, kinder, and friendlier because of your relationship with Jesus, or do you behave in pretty much the same way that you would if you had never heard of Him? Hopefully you're a better person because of the things you've learned from the Bible.

The world can be a confusing place. And sometimes you'll be tempted to misbehave. The next time you're tempted, slow down and remember the lessons you learn from the Bible. God's Word will keep you safe if you use it. Your job, of course, is to use it all day, every day.

☞ Remember This

Good behavior pays off. Bad behavior doesn't. Act accordingly.

✳ ✳ ✳

64
Be Cheerful!

A joyful heart is good medicine,
but a broken spirit dries up the bones.

PROVERBS 17:22 HCSB

The Bible teaches us that a cheerful heart is like medicine: it makes us feel better. And since God wants the best for all of us, we can be sure that He wants us to be cheerful and contented. So let's be thankful to God for His blessings, and let's share good cheer wherever we go.

Today, share kind words and friendly smiles with as many people as you can. The world needs all the cheering up it can get...and so do your friends.

 **A Timely Tip**

If you look for reasons to be cheerful, you'll find them. So keep looking.

***

65
Too Much Screen Time?

Let us look only to Jesus, the One who began
our faith and who makes it perfect.

HEBREWS 12:2 NCV

How much time do you spend each day looking at a TV, or a computer, or a smartphone? An hour? Maybe two? One survey found that the average kid spends three hours a day watching television and seven hours of total screen time! Please don't be like the average kid in that survey.

If you're careful what you watch, a little screen time can be a good thing. But if you end up wasting lots of time on silly programs or games, you should power-down and find something better to do.

God wants you to spend your time wisely. Your parents do, too. And so should you. Time is simply too valuable to waste.

***

Distractions must be conquered or they will conquer us.

A. W. TOZER

* * *

66
In Search of Answers

*You will seek Me and find Me
when you search for Me with all your heart.*

JEREMIAH 29:13 HCSB

God always hears your prayers, and He always answers them, too. What God does not do is this: He does not always answer your prayers as soon as you might like, and He does not always answer your prayers by saying yes.

God answers prayers, not according to our wishes, but according to His master plan. We don't know that plan, but we do know the Planner. And we must trust Him, even when we don't know exactly what the Lord is doing.

Are you praying? Then you can be sure God is listening. And you can be sure that His answer will arrive someday, maybe sooner than you think.

* * *

*The story of every great Christian achievement
is the history of answered prayer.*

E. M. BOUNDS

* * *

67
What's Really Important

A pretentious, showy life is an empty life;
a plain and simple life is a full life.

PROVERBS 13:7 MSG

Lots of people spend too much time worrying about the things they own. But if you're smart, you won't spend too much time worrying about stuff.

The Bible teaches this important lesson: it's not good to be too concerned about money or the stuff that money can buy. So take a lesson from God's Word and don't worry too much about the things you can buy in stores. Worry more about obeying your parents and obeying your heavenly Father—that's what's really important.

🖑 Remember This

The things you own aren't nearly as important as the person you're becoming.

* * *
68
The 23rd Psalm

The twenty-third psalm teaches us that God always protects us. It is one of the most beloved chapters in the Bible. You may not be able to memorize it in a single day, but if you keep trying you'll eventually know these verses by heart.

The LORD is my shepherd;
I shall not want.
He makes me to lie down in green pastures;
He leads me beside the still waters.
He restores my soul;
He leads me in the paths of righteousness
For His name's sake.

Yea, though I walk through the valley of the shadow of death,
I will fear no evil;
For You are with me;
Your rod and Your staff, they comfort me.

You prepare a table before me in the presence of my enemies;
You anoint my head with oil;
My cup runs over.
Surely goodness and mercy shall follow me
All the days of my life;
And I will dwell in the house of the LORD
Forever. (NKJV)

✳ ✳ ✳

69
God Is Always Watching

The LORD sees everything you do, and he watches where you go.

PROVERBS 5:21 NCV

If we misbehave, God knows. Even when we think nobody is watching, God is. There's nothing we can do that escapes His view.

If you're old enough to know right from wrong, then you're old enough to do something about it. In other words, you should always try to do the right thing, and you should also do your very best to avoid making big mistakes.

When you slow down and think before you act, you can make better decisions. So here's some good advice: before you make an important choice, slow down long enough to remember that God is watching. When you do, you'll make the right decision every time.

☞ Remember This

God wants you to behave yourself, and He's always watching. The rest is up to you.

***

70
Study God's Word

As newborn babies want milk, you should want the pure and simple teaching. By it you can grow mature in your salvation.

1 Peter 2:2 NCV

What book contains everything that God has to say about His rules and His Son? The Bible, of course. If you read the Bible every day, you'll soon learn how God wants you to behave.

Since doing the right thing (and the smart thing) is important to God, it should be important to you, too. And you'll learn what's right by reading His holy Word.

The Bible is the most important book you'll ever own. It's God's instruction book. Read it every day, and follow the instructions. When you do, you'll be safe now and forever.

***

*Wise people listen to wise instruction,
especially instruction from the Word of God.*

Warren Wiersbe

71

Trust Your Heavenly Father

If God is for us, who is against us?

ROMANS 8:31 HCSB

God always keeps His promises. That's why you should trust Him to handle everything, including your worries, your problems, your fears, and your future.

God has big plans for you. And He has promised to protect you now and throughout eternity. The Lord is your Shepherd today and throughout eternity—His love lasts forever. Trust the Shepherd.

✳ ✳ ✳

If you learn to trust God with a child-like dependence on Him as your loving heavenly Father, no trouble can destroy you.

BILLY GRAHAM

72
Show Respect for Everybody

Do to others as you would have them do to you.

LUKE 6:31 NIV

In the eyes of the Lord, all people are important, so we should treat them that way. Of course it's easy to be nice to the people we want to impress, but what about everybody else?

Jesus gave us clear instructions: He said that we should treat everybody in the same way that we want to be treated. And since we want respect from other people, we should treat them with respect, too. No exceptions.

＊＊＊

*If my heart is right with God,
every human being is my neighbor.*

OSWALD CHAMBERS

✳ ✳ ✳

73

Patience and Trust

Trust in him at all times, O people;
pour out your hearts to him, for God is our refuge.

PSALM 62:8 NIV

Usually, we know what we want and we know when we want it: *now*. We want our problems solved promptly; we want our questions answered quickly; and we want our dreams to come true immediately! But sometimes God has other plans, so we must be patient.

Psalm 37:7 commands us to "rest in the LORD, and wait patiently for Him" (NKJV). But for most of us, waiting quietly for God is difficult. Difficult, but not impossible.

So, the next time you find yourself waiting impatiently for the Lord to make your dreams come true, slow down, take a deep breath, and remember that God's timing is perfect. And remember that sometimes the best thing you can do is to wait patiently and trust the Lord.

✳ ✳ ✳

Be patient. God is using today's difficulties to strengthen
you for tomorrow. He is equipping you.
The God who makes things grow will help you bear fruit.

MAX LUCADO

✷✷✷

74
His Promises Never Fail

Let us hold tightly without wavering to the hope we affirm, for God can be trusted to keep his promise.

HEBREWS 10:23 NLT

When the Lord makes a promise, He always keeps it. So when you read something in the Bible, you can be sure that it's true.

Think about some of the amazing promises that God has made to you. He's promised to love you and protect you. He's promised to listen carefully to your prayers. And, He's promised that if you welcome His Son into your heart, you'll live happily forever in heaven.

So the next time you're worried or afraid, remind yourself of the promises that never fail: God's promises. When you do, you'll know that you are protected today, tomorrow, and forever.

✷✷✷

There are four words I wish we would never forget, and they are, "God keeps His word."

CHARLES SWINDOLL

75
It's Fun to Give and Serve

Enjoy serving the LORD,
and he will give you what you want.

PSALM 37:4 NCV

When the offering plate passes by, are you old enough to drop anything in it? If you are, congratulations! But if you're not quite old enough to give money to the church, don't worry—there are still lots of ways you can help What are some things you can share? For starters, you can share your smile, your laughter, your cooperation, your prayers, and your love. You can be helpful and you can behave yourself. And you can show other kids what it means to be a good Christian.

Even if you don't have lots of money, there are still plenty of ways you can give and serve. And, the best time to start giving and serving is now.

✳ ✳ ✳

Christianity is not a spectator sport;
it is something in which we become totally involved.

BILLY GRAHAM

76
Always Tell the Truth

But when the Spirit of truth comes,
he will lead you into all truth.

JOHN 16:13 NCV

Sometimes telling the truth can be hard. That's when it's tempting to tell a lie. But even when telling the truth is hard, it's still easier—and better—to tell the truth than it is to live with the consequences of telling a lie.

Telling a lie can be easier in the beginning, but it's always harder in the end! In the end, when people find out that you've been untruthful, *they* may feel hurt and *you* will feel embarrassed.

So make this promise to yourself, and keep it: always tell the truth from the start. You'll be doing yourself a big favor, and you'll be obeying the Word of God.

✳ ✳ ✳

Truth will triumph. The Father of truth will win,
and the followers of truth will be saved.

MAX LUCADO

✳ ✳ ✳

77
Lies Can Lead to Trouble

Lying lips are detestable to the LORD.

PROVERBS 12:22 HCSB

Lies can lead to trouble, lots of trouble. That's why God wants us to tell the truth, even when it's hard.

When we're dishonest, we make ourselves unhappy in surprising ways. We feel guilty because we know that we've disappointed God. And to make matters worse, the truth usually comes out anyway! So it's easy to see that lies always cause more problems than they solve.

Happiness and honesty always go hand in hand. But it's up to you to make sure that *you* go hand in hand with them!

✳ ✳ ✳

A lie is like a snowball: the further you roll it, the bigger it becomes.

MARTIN LUTHER

*** * ***

78
Actions Speak Louder

In every way be an example of doing good deeds.
When you teach, do it with honesty and seriousness.

TITUS 2:7 NCV

How can people know that you're a Christian? You can tell them so, and that's a good thing. Talking about your faith is important. But telling people about Jesus isn't enough. You should also show people how a Christian (like you) should behave.

God knows that, as the old saying goes, "Actions speak louder than words." And He wants you to be a shining example for the world to see. Then, when another person sees how you behave, that person will know what it means to be a good Christian...a good Christian like you!

Remember This

As a Christian, the most important light you shine is the light that your own life shines on other people. Let your light shine brightly today and every day.

79
Forgive and Forget

Smart people know how to hold their tongue;
their grandeur is to forgive and forget.

PROVERBS 19:11 MSG

Have you heard the old saying "Forgive and forget"? Well, it's certainly easier said than done. It's easy to talk about forgiving somebody, but actually forgiving that person can be much harder. And when it comes to forgetting, forget about it!

"Forgive and forget" is good advice, and it works sometimes. But on other occasions, when we've been hurt badly, it's impossible to forget the pain. Yet even when we can't forget, we can forgive. And that's exactly what God teaches us to do.

☞ Remember This

When you forgive other people, you'll feel better about your world and yourself.

✳ ✳ ✳

80
Your Best Friend

I am the good shepherd.
The good shepherd gives His life for the sheep.

JOHN 10:11 NKJV

Jesus is your very best friend. In fact, He did an amazing thing for you: He gave up His life so that you can live forever with Him in heaven.

Christ's love is always free and it never grows old. It's an incredible gift that you can never fully repay. But what you can do is this: you can tell other people about Jesus. When you do, you'll show the world how much Christ's love means to you. And that's exactly what your very best friend wants you to do.

Jesus departed from our sight that he might return
to our hearts. He departed, and behold, he is here.

ST. AUGUSTINE

✳ ✳ ✳

81
The Fruit of the Spirit

But the fruit of the Spirit is love, joy, peace, patience,
kindness, goodness, faith, gentleness, self-control.
Against such things there is no law.

GALATIANS 5:22–23 HCSB

In the Bible we are told that Christians who "live by the Spirit" will bear the "fruit of the Spirit."

What, exactly, is the fruit of the Spirit? It's a way of behaving yourself, a way of treating other people, a way of showing the world what it means to follow Christ.

Will you try to be patient, joyful, loving, and kind? Will you learn to control yourself? And while you're at it, will you praise God for the blessings He's given you? If so, you'll show everybody that the fruit of the Spirit can make a wonderful difference in the life of a very good Christian: you!

☞ Remember This

When you love God and obey His teachings, you'll make His world and your world a much better place.

* * *

82
When You Help Other People, You Feel Better about Yourself

So let us try to do what makes peace and helps one another.

ROMANS 14:19 NCV

Here's a simple way to feel better about yourself: help somebody. When you help another person, you know that you're obeying God, and that will make you feel better. But it doesn't stop there. When you help someone in need, you're also showing other kids what it means to be a Christian. That means you're following in Christ's footsteps, and you should feel good about that, too.

So the next time you get the chance to help someone, don't delay. You'll make two people happy.

☞ Remember This

When you help other people, you'll know that you've obeyed God, and He'll know it, too.

***

83
Caring for Your Family

Love must be without hypocrisy. Detest evil; cling to what is good. Show family affection to one another with brotherly love. Outdo one another in showing honor.

ROMANS 12:9–10 HCSB

Do you care for your family? Of course you do. Your family is God's gift to you, and it's up to you to treat that gift with respect, with honor, and with love.

The Bible teaches that love is a "fruit of the Spirit." So make sure that everybody in your family can see—by your actions and by your words—that the spirit of love continues to grow in your heart. When you do, you'll make everybody happy, including that boy you see every time you look in the mirror.

👉 Remember This

Your family is a gift from God. Treat it with care.

84
Be Friendly

*It is good and pleasant when God's people
live together in peace!*

PSALM 133:1 NCV

The Bible tells us that a true friendship is a wonderful thing. That's why it's good to know how to make and keep good friends.

If you want to make lots of friends, practice the Golden Rule with everybody you know. Be kind. Share. Say nice things. Be helpful. When you do, you'll discover that the Golden Rule isn't just a nice way to behave; it's also a great way to make and to keep friends!

👉 Remember This

The number-one rule of friendship is the Golden one.

✳ ✳ ✳

85
Faith Heals

*Jesus turned around, and when he saw her he said,
"Daughter, be encouraged! Your faith has made you well."
And the woman was healed at that moment.*

MATTHEW 9:22 NLT

Faith can heal a broken heart or a broken body. When a suffering woman sought healing by merely touching the hem of His cloak, Jesus informed her that her faith had restored her health. It was a miracle that happened long ago, but miracles still happen every day.

When you place your faith in the hands of Jesus, you'll be amazed at the miraculous things He can do. So build your faith through prayer, through worship, and through Bible study. And trust God's plans. With Him, all things are possible, and He stands ready to do wonderful things for you *if* you have faith.

✳ ✳ ✳

*Faith is the assurance that the thing which
God has said in His Word is true, and that God
will act according to what He has said.*

GEORGE MUELLER

***

86
Today Is Your Classroom

Above all and before all, do this: Get Wisdom!
Write this at the top of your list: Get Understanding!
PROVERBS 4:7 MSG

Today, like every other day, can be your classroom. So what will you learn? Will you listen carefully to your parents, to your grandparents, to your teachers, and to your pastor? And will read your Bible every day, not just on Sundays? If you answer these questions with a great big yes, then you'll become a very smart person.

Learning is fun. And the more things you learn, the better your life will be. So, try to learn something new every day, starting now.

 A Timely Tip

You can learn something new every day...and you should!

***

87
It's Good to Have Friends Who Behave Themselves

Walk with the wise and become wise;
associate with fools and get in trouble.

Proverbs 13:20 NLT

It's good to have friends who behave themselves. Why? Because when your friends act like Christians, it's easier for you to act like a Christian, too.

Of course, sometimes you may find yourself in a situation where people are misbehaving. When the people around you are behaving badly, you may be tempted to go along with the crowd. But if the crowd is going in the wrong direction, it's not right to join in; it's time to join another crowd.

Are you a people-pleaser or a God-pleaser? Hopefully you've figured out that it's more important to please the Lord than it is to please misbehaving friends. No exceptions.

***

The best evidence of our having the truth
is our walking in the truth.

Matthew Henry

✳ ✳ ✳

88
Watch What You Watch

Don't depend on your own wisdom.
Respect the LORD and refuse to do wrong.
PROVERBS 3:7 NCV

There are lots of fun things to watch on TV. And you can certainly play games or watch shows on a smartphone, too. But not everything you see on a TV screen or a smartphone is good for you. So please careful about the things you watch!

Your parents can tell you which shows are good for you and which ones aren't. When they tell you not to watch something, please don't be upset. Your parents are simply trying to protect you from harm. Instead of being angry, you should thank them—they're not being mean; they're just being good parents.

 **A Timely Tip**

There are a few TV shows worth watching. There are many that aren't worth watching. So be careful what you watch. And when in doubt, let your parents decide.

* * *

89
Be Joyful!

Rejoice in the Lord always. I will say it again: Rejoice!

PHILIPPIANS 4:4 HCSB

God wants you to rejoice. A joyful life starts with a joyful attitude. So when you're feeling tired or sad, here's something to remember: This day is a gift from God. And it's up to you to celebrate God's gift by being cheerful, helpful, courteous, and well-behaved. How can you do these things? A good place to start is by doing your best to think good thoughts.

God wants you to have a happy, joyful life, but that doesn't mean that you'll be happy all the time. Sometimes you may not feel like feeling happy, and when you don't, you should talk to your parents about your emotions. When you talk things over with your parents, you'll feel better, and they'll feel better, too.

* * *

Joy is the direct result of having God's perspective on our daily lives and the effect of loving our Lord enough to obey His commands and trust His promises.

BILL BRIGHT

* * *

90
It's Good to Be Generous

The one who blesses others is abundantly blessed;
those who help others are helped.

PROVERBS 11:25 MSG

The Bible teaches us that God loves—and blesses—a cheerful giver. But sometimes it's tempting to be selfish. It's tempting to want to keep everything for yourself, and it's tempting to say, "No, that's MINE!" But it's better to say, "I'll share it with you."

Are you sometimes tempted to say, "I don't want to share that!"—and then do you feel a little sorry that you said it? If that sounds like you, don't worry—everybody is tempted to be selfish. But please resist that temptation. When you're generous, you'll make your parents proud and you'll make your Father in heaven proud, too. So remember this: it's good to be generous.

* * *

If you want to be truly happy, you won't find it on
an endless quest for more stuff. You'll find it in receiving
God's generosity and in passing that generosity along.

BILL HYBELS

✳✳✳
91
Plan Ahead

The plans of hard-working people earn a profit,
but those who act too quickly become poor.

PROVERBS 21:5 NCV

The Bible teaches us to think carefully and to plan ahead. God wants us to behave wisely and knows that the better we plan, the better decisions we'll make.

Maybe you've heard the old saying "Haste makes waste." Well, that saying may be old, but it still applies to you. So, before you hastily jump into something new, take time to think things over. Otherwise, you might be sorry.

When you plan ahead, you'll make better choices. So think about the consequences of your actions before you do something silly...or dangerous...or both.

✳✳✳

Success and happiness are not destinations.
They are exciting, never-ending journeys.

ZIG ZIGLAR

* * *

92
Obey the Lord

When all has been heard, the conclusion of the matter is:
fear God and keep His commands.

ECCLESIASTES 12:13 HCSB

You have a choice to make: are you going to obey God's rules or not? It's a decision that you must make for yourself.

If you decide to behave yourself, you've made a smart choice. If you decide to obey your parents, you've made another smart choice. If you decide to pay attention to your teachers, you've made yet another good choice. And if you decide to obey God, you've made the very best choice of all.

So today and every day, obey all the rules, starting with God's rules. It's the smart way to behave and the best way to live.

* * *

The ultimate response to Jesus' teaching
is belief and obedience.

JOHN MACARTHUR

* * *

93
God Can Handle It

Now the God of all grace, who called you
to His eternal glory in Christ Jesus, will personally restore,
establish, strengthen, and support you.

1 PETER 5:10 HCSB

Whatever the size of your problem, God is bigger. And the Bible promises that He will protect you if you ask Him to. If you have a problem, God can handle it.

When you're worried, God can give you strength; if you're sad, God can give you comfort; if you're discouraged, God can give you hope. He is not just near; He is here. He is your Shepherd, so there's no need to worry. And that's a promise you can depend on, today and every day.

* * *

When you fall and skin your knees
and skin your heart, He'll pick you up.

CHARLES STANLEY

It's Good to Praise God

So that at the name of Jesus every knee will bow—
of those who are in heaven and on earth and under the earth—
and every tongue should confess that Jesus Christ is Lord,
to the glory of God the Father.

PHILIPPIANS 2:10–11 HCSB

It pays to praise God. But if you're like most kids, you feel like you don't have a minute to spare. From morning until night, you're busy doing things, learning things, watching things, and playing games. But no matter how busy you are—even if your schedule seems completely full—you should still slow down and say "thank You," to the Lord.

God has given you more blessings than you can count, and you owe Him everything—including your praise—starting right now and ending never.

✳ ✳ ✳

No matter what our circumstance,
we can find a reason to be thankful.

DAVID JEREMIAH

95

The Trouble with Gossip

A useless person causes trouble,
and a gossip ruins friendships.

PROVERBS 16:28 NCV

Do you know what gossip is? It's when we say bad things about people who are not around. When we gossip, we hurt the people we're talking about and we hurt ourselves. That's why the Bible tells us that gossip is wrong.

Sometimes it's tempting to talk about other people and say unkind things about them. But before long, the bad things we say come back to hurt us, and everybody loses. So if you want to be a kind person and a good friend, don't gossip, and don't listen to people who do.

 A Timely Tip

Avoiding gossip is simple: don't say something behind a person's back that you wouldn't want that person to hear.

✳ ✳ ✳
96
It's Good to Have Self-Control

Supplement your faith with a generous provision of moral excellence, and moral excellence with knowledge, and knowledge with self-control, and self-control with patient endurance, and patient endurance with godliness.

2 PETER 1:6 NLT

Sometimes we make choices without thinking very much about the consequences. That's when we can get ourselves into trouble.

The more self-control you have, the easier it is to make good choices and the easier it is to behave yourself. Why? Because when you learn to think first and do things next, you avoid lots of silly mistakes. So here's great advice: first, slow down long enough to figure out the right thing to do—and then do it. You'll make better decisions, and you'll be rewarded for your good choices and your good deeds.

☞ Remember This

If you can learn to control yourself, other people won't have to.

❋ ❋ ❋

97
God Has Given You Amazing Gifts

Thanks be to God for his indescribable gift!

2 CORINTHIANS 9:15 NIV

All people have special gifts—special blessings from God—and you are no exception. God has given you these talents for a reason: He wants you to use them. So today, make a promise to yourself that you will make the most of the talents that God has given you. Then keep improving those talents and making them grow. Then, when you're ready, share your gifts with the world. After all, the best way to say "thank You" for God's gifts is to use them.

 A Timely Tip

What you are is God's gift to you. What you become is your gift to God.

✳ ✳ ✳

98
Guard Your Heart

Guard your heart above all else, for it is the source of life.

PROVERBS 4:23 HCSB

The Lord loves you, and He wants the very best for you. He also wants you to be protected from the dangers and troubles of this world. So, God wants you to guard your heart.

Every day you make choices—lots of them. When you're about to make an important decision, your mind and your heart will usually tell you the right choice to make. And if you listen to your parents, they'll help you, too, by teaching you God's rules. When you've learned His rules—and when you obey them—you'll guard your heart and the Lord will bless you now and forever.

☞ Remember This

God wants you to think carefully about the things you do and the friends you make. When you make the right kind of friends, and when you take good care of yourself, you'll guard your heart, and you'll be blessed.

✳ ✳ ✳

99
The Best Policy

In every way be an example of doing good deeds.

TITUS 2:7 NCV

Honesty has been called "the best policy," but more importantly, it's God's policy. That means that you should always tell the truth. But nobody can tell the truth for you. You're the one who decides what you are going to say. You're the one who decides whether your words will be truthful or not.

If you want to have friends you can trust, you need to be a friend they can trust. And, if you want to live a life that is pleasing to God, you must make honesty a habit. When you do, everybody wins, especially you!

 A Timely Tip

Honesty is the best policy. Make sure that it's your policy, even when telling the truth makes you feel a little uncomfortable.

✳ ✳ ✳

100
Praise God

Let the godly sing for joy to the LORD;
it is fitting for the pure to praise him.

PSALM 33:1 NLT

The Bible teaches us that we should say "thank You" to the Lord. But sometimes we may not feel like thanking anybody, not even our Father in heaven.

When you stop to think about it, God has been very generous with you. So make sure that you express your thanks to Him as often as you can. And don't just praise the Lord on Sunday mornings. Praise Him every day, starting with this one.

☞ **Remember This**

The best moment to praise God is always the present one.

* * *

101
Put God First

You must not have any other god but me.

EXODUS 20:3 NLT

Sometimes it's hard to put God ahead of other things. After all, there are so many things that grab out attention. But the Lord wants us to love Him first, and He wants us to obey Him first. No exceptions.

When the Pharisees quizzed Jesus about God's most important commandment, Jesus answered, "Love the Lord your God with all your heart, all your soul, and all your mind. This is the first and most important command" (Matthew 22:37–38 NCV). So if you want to do the right thing, always put God in the place He deserves: first place.

☞ Remember This

God wants first place in your heart, and you deserve the experience of putting Him there. So don't wait another minute. Put God first today and every day.

102
Returning God's Love... By Sharing It

My dear, dear friends, if God loved us like this,
we certainly ought to love each other.

1 John 4:11 MSG

God loves you, and you should love Him. But that's not all—you should also love your family, your friends, and everybody else who crosses your path.

The Bible teaches us that God's love is wonderful, and it lasts forever. So, how much does God love you? His love for you is so huge that you can't really figure it out. But even if you can't completely understand God's love, you can feel it…and you can share it…today!

☞ Remember This

God loves you very much, and He wants you to love other people. When you're kind, courteous, and helpful, you'll be glad, and God will be glad, too.

✳ ✳ ✳

103
God's Love Never Ends

We know how much God loves us, and we have
put our trust in his love. God is love, and all who live
in love live in God, and God lives in them.

1 JOHN 4:16 NLT

The Bible teaches us that God is love. And it says that if we wish to know God, we must have love in our hearts. Sometimes, of course, when we're tired, angry, or frustrated, it is hard to be kind. Thankfully, frustration and anger are feelings that come and go, but the Lord's love lasts forever.

Today and every day, share God's love with your family and friends. When you share God's love, you make your corner of the world a happier place. And you make God happy, too.

👉 Remember This

God loves you today and every day. And that's exactly how often you should share His love with family and friends: today and every day.

※ ※ ※

104
God's Timing Is Best

He has made everything appropriate in its time.
He has also put eternity in their hearts, but man cannot
discover the work God has done from beginning to end.

ECCLESIASTES 3:11 HCSB

Sometimes it's hard to wait for the things we want. We want things to happen now, not later, and we're always in a hurry to get the things we want.

If you're waiting impatiently for something you want very badly, please remember that God's timing is best. He knows exactly what you need and exactly when you need it. So trust your heavenly Father, and be patient. And remember that Father always knows best.

※ ※ ※

Will not the Lord's time be better than your time?

C. H. SPURGEON

✳ ✳ ✳

105
Giving an Account of Ourselves

Yes, each of us will give a personal account to God.
ROMANS 14:12 NLT

God knows everything about us. And the Bible teaches us that someday we'll all have to talk to the Lord about the things we've done and the way we've behaved.

God doesn't expect us to be perfect, but He does want us to follow Jesus. And He wants us to obey the rules that we find in the Holy Bible.

So if you want to have a happy conversation on that fateful day when you give an accounting of yourself to the Lord, welcome Jesus into your heart and obey God's rules. It's the best way—and the safest way—to live.

☞ Remember This

God is watching everything you do. So try hard to avoid the things He doesn't approve of.

※ ※ ※

106
Be Patient with Other People

God has chosen you and made you his holy people.
He loves you. So you should always clothe yourselves with
mercy, kindness, humility, gentleness, and patience.

COLOSSIANS 3:12 NCV

Jesus gave us a Golden Rule that we must never forget. He taught us to treat other people in the same way that we want to be treated. And because we want other people to be patient with us, we, in turn, should be patient with them.

Sometimes, it's hard to be patient, but we've got to do our best. And when we do, we're following the Golden Rule—God's rule for how to treat others—and everybody wins!

※ ※ ※

The next time you're disappointed,
don't panic and don't give up. Just be patient
and let God remind you he's still in control.

MAX LUCADO

107
You're One-of-a-Kind

You made my whole being...praise you because
you made me in an amazing and wonderful way.
What you have done is wonderful. I know this very well.

PSALM 139:13–14 NCV

There's nobody else in the world who's exactly like you. You're one-of-a-kind, and that makes you very special indeed. And you're also special because God loves you. The Lord cares for you, and He will never leave you, not even for a moment.

So, take time today to think about what it means to be the only person in the whole world with your unique talents, experiences, and opportunities. And while you're at it, take time to thank God for all He has done. You're His beloved child today, tomorrow, and forever.

If you ever put a price tag on yourself, it would have to read "Jesus" because that is what God paid to save you.

JOSH MCDOWELL

✳ ✳ ✳

108
God's Way Is the Right Way

There is no wisdom, understanding,
or advice that can succeed against the LORD.

PROVERBS 21:30 NCV

God knows what's best for you, and He knows the right path for you to take. But He won't force you to follow His will. He lets you make choices on your own.

Do you want to become the kind of Christian that God intends for you to be? It's up to you! You'll be the one who will decide how you behave.

If you obey God and follow in the footsteps of His Son, you will be rewarded now and forever. So guard your heart and trust your heavenly Father. He knows the right way, and He will never lead you astray.

👉 Remember This

Sometimes people can lead you down a wrong path, but God never will. So, if you're about to make an important choice, trust God. His way is always the right way.

* * *
109
Be a Good Example

Do not let anyone treat you as if you are unimportant because you are young. Instead, be an example to the believers with your words, your actions, your love, your faith, and your pure life.

1 Timothy 4:12 NCV

Maybe you think that because you're young, you don't need to worry about setting a good example for others to follow. Well, if you think that, you're wrong. God wants people of all ages, including people of your age, to shine brightly for Him.

This world already has enough bad examples. What it needs is more good examples, more people who are willing to follow in Christ's footsteps and show their friends what it means to be a good person and a good Christian. You can be a great example to your friends and family. And that's exactly what God wants you to do. So don't delay…be a good example today!

☞ Remember This

The world needs good examples. And God wants you to be a good example. So don't delay: be a good example today.

110
Learning How to Be More Patient

*God blesses those who patiently endure testing
and temptation. Afterward they will receive the crown
of life that God has promised to those who love him.*

JAMES 1:12 NLT

If you try, you can learn to be a more patient person. And that's a lesson God wants you to learn. He wants you to behave wisely, and that takes patience.

The dictionary defines the word patience as "the ability to be calm." When you're patient, it means that you've learned to control your emotions before your emotions take control of you.

If you can stay calm and be patient, you'll be the kind of person whose good deeds are a blessing to your family and friends. And that's exactly the kind of person that God wants you to be.

☞ Remember This

If you want to become a more patient person, ask God to help you. He can help you learn ways to slow down and calm down.

* * *

111
Jesus Lives!

He is not here, but He has been resurrected!

Luke 24:6 HCSB

Jesus died on a cross and was buried in a tomb. On the third day, He rose from the dead. It's called "the resurrection," and we celebrate it every year on Easter Sunday.

The story of Easter is the story of God's love, God's miracles, and God's offer of eternal life to all people who welcome Jesus into their hearts.

As we think about Christ's resurrection and what it means to us, we should pause and give thanks to the Father and the Son for the gift of eternal life, a gift that costs us so little because it cost Christ so much.

* * *

The resurrection of Jesus, the whole alphabet of human hope, is the heart of the gospel.

R. G. Lee

* * *

112
Be a Servant

Whoever serves me must follow me.
Then my servant will be with me everywhere I am.
My Father will honor anyone who serves me.

JOHN 12:26 NCV

Jesus said that if we want to follow Him, we must serve Him. How? By serving people who need our help. Jesus wants us to become humble servants for Him.

Sometime soon you'll have a chance to help someone. When that time comes, remember that Jesus wants you to be kind and generous. Jesus was a servant to all mankind. Now it's your turn. It is through service to others that you can show people what it really means to follow Christ.

* * *

Service is the pathway to real significance.
RICK WARREN

***

113
Your Future Is Very Bright!

Wisdom is pleasing to you.
If you find it, you have hope for the future.

How can you make smart choices if you're unwilling to trust God and obey Him? The answer, of course, is that you can't. That's why you should trust God in everything (and that means entrusting your future to Him, too).

How bright is your future? Well, if you're a faithful believer in Christ, your future is incredibly bright, now and forever. So today, as you live in the present and look to the future, remember that God has an amazing plan for you. Act—and believe—accordingly.

***

The Christian believes in a fabulous future.

* * *

114
God's Love

*For the LORD your God is living among you. He is a mighty
savior. He will take delight in you with great gladness.
With his love, he will calm all your fears.
He will rejoice over you with joyful songs.*

ZEPHANIAH 3:17 NLT

The Lord loves you, and He wants the best for you.
His amazing love never ends. No matter where you are
(and no matter what you've done), you're never beyond
the reach of His forgiveness. He is always willing to teach
you, to guide you, and to protect you.

So take time today (and every day) to thank the Lord
for a love that is too big to understand with your head but
not too big to feel with your heart. Accept His love and
share it, now and forever.

* * *

*Love, for instance, is not something God has which may
grow or diminish or cease to be. His love is the way God is,
and when He loves He is simply being Himself.*

A. W. TOZER

115
Think before You Speak

*Watch the way you talk. Let nothing foul or dirty come out
of your mouth. Say only what helps, each word a gift.*

EPHESIANS 4:29 MSG

Your words have the power to help people or hurt them.
That's why you must learn to think before you speak.
And, since you want other people to say kind things to
you, you should say kind things to them, too.

Today and every day, make sure that you say helpful
things, not hurtful things. You'll feel better about yourself
when you help other people feel better about themselves.

When you think before you speak, you choose your
words wisely. Everybody needs to hear kind words, and
that's exactly the kind of words they should hear from you!

The great test of a man's character is his tongue.

OSWALD CHAMBERS

116
Be Hopeful!

Let's keep a firm grip on the promises that keep us going.
He always keeps his word.

HEBREWS 10:23 MSG

Are you a hope-filled boy? Hopefully so!

When you stop to think about it, you have many reasons to be hopeful: God loves you, your family loves you, Jesus loves you, and you've got a very bright future ahead of you. So trust God, follow His Son, say your prayers, do your work, and be hopeful. When you do these things, you'll be happier; you'll be healthier; you'll be more successful; and—most importantly—you'll feel closer to God.

☞ Remember This

Be hopeful. You and God, working together, can do amazing things.

✳ ✳ ✳
117
Share Your Stuff

And God will generously provide all you need.
Then you will always have everything you need
and plenty left over to share with others.

2 Corinthians 9:8 NLT

Are you one of those boys who's lucky enough to have a closet filled with clothes, toys, and other stuff? If so, it's probably time to share some it.

When your mom or dad says it's time to clean your closet and give some things away, don't be disappointed. Instead of whining, think about all the kids who could enjoy the things that you don't use very much. And while you're at it, think about what Jesus might tell you to do if He were here. Jesus would tell you to give generously and cheerfully, and that's exactly what you should do.

☞ Remember This

God has given you many blessings, and He wants you to share them. So it's always a good time to share.

***

118
Listening to God

Speak, Lord. I am your servant and I am listening.

1 Samuel 3:10 NCV

How can you figure out what God wants you to do? The Lord is trying to get His message through to you, but it can be hard to hear Him sometimes, especially when the smartphone is on or the TV is blaring.

So if you want to hear from your Father in heaven, it helps to be quiet and pay attention. You should pay attention whenever you read your Bible. And, of course, you should always try to pay attention in church. And you should listen to your parents and your grandparents when they're telling you about God. When you do these things, you'll begin to figure out how the Lord wants you to behave. When you follow His instructions, you'll be glad you did!

👉 Remember This

God has important things to teach you. So, listen carefully to your conscience, pay attention to the things you learn in the Bible, and try to learn something new every day. When you do, God will guide you and protect you.

119
Use God's Golden Rule

Just as you want others to do for you, do the same for them.
LUKE 6:31 HCSB

How can you decide when helping another person is the right thing to do? One way is to let the Golden Rule be your guide. Simply treat the other person as you'd want to be treated if you were in his—or her—situation. If you're pretty sure that you'd like a helping hand, then give the other person a helping hand.

God wants everybody to be helpful and kind. Whenever you do a good deed, the Lord is pleased. So when other people need your help, be quick to be kind. It's the right thing to do and the best way to live.

☞ Remember This

When you obey the Golden Rule, you'll make everybody happy, including yourself. So don't delay; obey the Golden Rule today and every day.

120
This World Is Not Your Real Home

*Do not love the world or the things that belong to the world.
If anyone loves the world, love for the Father is not in him.*

1 JOHN 2:15 HCSB

There's an old hymn that contains these words: "This world is not my home; I'm just passing through." These words are true, thank goodness! This crazy world can be filled with headaches and trouble. Thankfully, your real home is heaven, a place where you can live forever with Jesus.

Jesus promises us that He has overcome the troubles of this world. We must trust Him, and we must obey His commandments. When we do, we are forever blessed by the Son of God and by His Father in heaven.

*The only ultimate disaster that can befall us, I have come
to realize, is to feel ourselves to be home on earth.*

MAX LUCADO

✳ ✳ ✳

121
Be a Cheerful Giver

God loves that person who gives cheerfully.

2 CORINTHIANS 9:7 NLT

The Bible teaches that it's better to be generous than selfish, but sometimes you may not feel like sharing your things. When you feel that way, you'll be tempted to keep everything for yourself. But God has a better plan.

God wants you to share the things you have with people who are less fortunate than you are. So, the next time you have a chance to be a cheerful giver, be glad. It's good to be generous.

When you share your blessings, God will be pleased with you, and you'll be pleased with yourself. So do yourself (and everybody else) a favor: be a cheerful giver today and every day.

👉 Remember This

If you give something away, do it cheerfully. God loves a cheerful giver.

* * *

122
Getting to Know God

*You shall love the LORD your God with all your heart
and with all your soul and with all your might.*

DEUTERONOMY 6:5 NASB

Want to know God better? Then talk to Him every day.

Each day has 1,440 minutes—will you spend a few of those minutes with your heavenly Father? He deserves that much of your time and more.

The Lord wants to teach you and guide you. And you have lots to learn. So, if you haven't already done so, form the habit of spending time with Him—and reading your Bible—every day. No exceptions.

 **A Timely Tip**

When you spend some time with God every day, you'll be happier, healthier, and smarter. Plus, you'll make better decisions. So let the Bible be your guide today and every day.

∗ ∗ ∗

123
It's Good to Be Patient

Patience is better than strength.
Controlling your temper is better than capturing a city.
PROVERBS 16:32 NCV

In the book of Proverbs, King Solomon had some valuable advice. He warned that impatience and anger lead only to trouble.

The next time you're tempted to say an unkind word or to strike out in anger, remember Solomon. He was one of the wisest men who ever lived, and he knew that it's better to be patient. So remain calm, control yourself, and remember that patience is best. After all, if it's good enough for a wise man like Solomon, it should be good enough for us, too.

☞ Remember This

Patience pays. Impatience costs. Behave accordingly.

✳ ✳ ✳
124
Give Thanks to God!

Give thanks to the LORD, for He is good;
His faithful love endures forever.

PSALM 106:1 HCSB

*A*re you a thankful person? You should be. After all, you have much to be thankful for. And who has given you all the wonderful things you enjoy? Your parents are responsible for many of those blessings, of course. But all of our blessings really start with God.

Today and every day, tell the Lord how grateful you are for His promises and for His gifts. Since you've been given so much, it's always the right time to say "thank You" to the One who has given you more blessings than you can count.

☞ Remember This

A small light will do a great deal when it is in a very dark place. Put one little tallow candle in the middle of a large hall, and it will give a great deal of light.

The best day to be thankful is this very day, and the best moment to praise God is this very moment.

***

125
Learning Life's Lessons...
the Easy Way

Whoever is stubborn after being corrected many times
will suddenly be hurt beyond cure.

You can learn life's lessons the easy way or the hard way. What's the easy way? Simple: When God teaches you a lesson, you learn it the first time. And what's the hard way? When God tries to teach you a lesson, you ignore Him the first time…and the second time…and the third time… You get the picture.

God has many things He wants to teach you, so keep your eyes, your ears, and your heart open. When you do, you'll learn new things every day, and you'll have fun doing it.

✳ ✳ ✳

While it is wise to learn from experience,
it is wiser to learn from the experience of others.

RICK WARREN

126
Keep Making Good Choices

But the path of the just is like the shining sun, that shines ever brighter unto the perfect day. The way of the wicked is like darkness; they do not know what makes them stumble.

PROVERBS 4:18–19 NKJV

Sometimes it's easier to do the wrong thing than to do the right thing, especially if we're angry or tired. But poor choices almost always leads to trouble, and fast.

When you do the right thing, you don't have to worry about what you did or what you said. But, when you do the wrong thing, you'll be worried that someone will find out. So do yourself—and everybody else—a favor: obey God and listen carefully to your conscience. When you know you've done the right thing, you'll feel better about yourself, and you'll make God happy, too.

✴✴✴

Be such a person, and live such a life,
that if every person were such as you, and every life
a life like yours, this earth would be God's Paradise.

PHILLIPS BROOKS

✳ ✳ ✳

127
Life Is Great!

Rejoice in the LORD, you righteous ones;
praise from the upright is beautiful.

PSALM 33:1 HCSB

Your life is a priceless, one-of-a-kind gift from God. Your job is to unwrap His gift, to use it wisely, and to give thanks to the Giver.

This day, like every other day, provides you with many opportunities to serve the Lord by following in the footsteps of His Son. Jesus brings joy to the world, and He can bring joy to your heart, too. So rejoice and be glad. This is the day the Lord has made. And it's a special gift that should be enjoyed and celebrated *by you*.

✳ ✳ ✳

Joy is the serious business of heaven.

C. S. LEWIS

✳✳✳
128
God's Instruction Book

Your word is a lamp for my feet and a light on my path.

PSALM 119:105 HCSB

God has given us a holy manual, a guidebook for life called the Holy Bible. It contains instructions that, if followed precisely, will lead to peace, happiness, and eternal life. But if we choose to ignore God's commandments, the results will be much different…and much worse.

Wherever you go, God is there, so make Him your traveling companion. Study His Word and live by it. Make your life a shining example for those who have not yet found Christ. Pray often, praise the Lord, and celebrate His blessings every day. When you do, you'll have a wonderful life.

And for further instructions, read the manual.

✳✳✳

God's Book is packed with overwhelming riches.

OSWALD CHAMBERS

*** ✳ ✳ ✳

129
If You're Worried, Talk Things Over

Anxiety in a man's heart weighs it down,
but a good word cheers it up.

PROVERBS 12:25 HCSB

When you're worried, there are two places you can go to talk things over. You can talk to the people who care about you, and you can talk to God.

When you have a problem, it helps to talk about it with parents, grandparents, and concerned adults. But you shouldn't stop there. You should also talk to God in prayer. If you're upset about something, you can pray about it any time you want. God is always listening, and He always wants to hear from you.

So when you're worried, try this plan: talk and pray. Talk to the grown-ups who love you, and pray to the heavenly Father who made you. The more you talk and the more you pray, the better you'll feel.

✳ ✳ ✳

Today is the tomorrow we worried about yesterday.

DENNIS SWANBERG

* * *
130
Know When to Say No

Good sense will protect you; understanding will guard you.
It will keep you from the wicked, from those whose words
are bad, who don't do what is right but what is evil.

When your friends misbehave, do you tell them to stop, or do you go along with the crowd? Usually it's easier to go along with the crowd—or to say nothing at all—but that's the wrong thing to do. It's better to stand up for what you know is right.

People who constantly misbehave can spoil things in a hurry. So if your friends behave poorly, just say no! And keep saying until either (1) your friends start behaving better, or (2) you find better friends!

👉 Remember This

If somebody wants you to do something that isn't right, say no. When your conscience says no, you must say no, too.

* * *

131
Choose to Be Kind

Therefore, God's chosen ones, holy and loved, put on heartfelt compassion, kindness, humility, gentleness, and patience.

COLOSSIANS 3:12 HCSB

Kindness is a choice. Sometimes, when we feel happy or hopeful, it's easy to be kind. Other times, when we're tired or sad, it's much harder to be kind. But the Bible teaches us to be kind, even when we don't feel like it.

So please do everybody (including yourself) a big favor: try to be kind all the time. It's the smart choice; it's the right thing to do; and it's the best way to live.

 **A Timely Tip**

Keep your eyes open wide and your heart open wider.

* * *

132
Trust the Quiet Voice Inside

In quietness and trust is your strength.

ISAIAH 30:15 NASB

You have a little voice in your head called your conscience. Your conscience is a feeling that tells you whether something is right or wrong—and it's a feeling that makes you feel better about yourself when you know you've done the right thing.

Your conscience is a gift from God, and it's an important tool. Pay attention to it! The more you listen to your conscience, the better choices you'll make. So the next time you're about to make a big decision, take this advice: first, slow down long enough to figure out the right thing to do—and then do it! When you pay careful attention to the quiet voice of your conscience, you'll be proud of yourself...and other people will be proud of you, too.

* * *

One of the ways God has revealed Himself to us is in the conscience. Conscience is God's lamp within our hearts.

BILLY GRAHAM

133
Avoid Arguments

An angry man starts fights;
a hot-tempered person commits all kinds of sin.
PROVERBS 29:22 NLT

*A*rguments seldom solve anything, but they can create plenty of problems. When we argue—or when we lose control of our emotions—we do things that we shouldn't do. Sometimes, we throw tantrums. How silly! Other times we whine or pout. So sad!

The Bible tells us that it is foolish to become angry and that it is wise to remain calm. That's why we should slow down and think before we speak.

Do you want to make life better for yourself and for your family? Then be patient and kind. And while you're at it, avoid arguments. It's the wise way to live.

 **A Timely Tip**

You don't have to attend every argument you're invited to!

* * *

134
You Can't Buy Happiness

We brought nothing into the world, so we can take nothing out.
But, if we have food and clothes, we will be satisfied with that.

1 TIMOTHY 6:7–8 NCV

Here's something to remember about stuff: It's not that important! Lots of people fall in love with money and the things that money can buy. But God cares about people, not possessions, and so must you.

You shouldn't be too worried about the clothes you wear, or the things you own. And above all, don't ever let your self-esteem depend upon the things that you (or your parents) own.

The stuff that you own isn't nearly as important as the love that you feel in your heart—love for your family, love for your friends, and love for your Father in heaven. So forget about stuff and focus, instead, on the things that really matter. When you do, you'll be glad, and God will be glad, too.

* * *

Order your soul; reduce your wants; associate in Christian
community; obey the laws; trust in Providence.

St. Augustine

✳ ✳ ✳

135
God Will Show You the Way

I will instruct you and show you the way to go;
with My eye on you, I will give counsel.

PSALM 32:8 HCSB

God has a wonderful plan for your life here on earth and for your life forever, with Him, in heaven. The Lord has also given you an amazing guidebook called the Holy Bible. If you read His Word, pray often, and listen to your parents and teachers, God will lead you on the right path: His path.

The Lord doesn't force you to follow His plan, and He doesn't make you behave yourself. He lets you make choices, and He hopes you choose wisely.

Today and every day, ask God to guide you. He wants to use you in wonderful, unexpected ways. Your job, of course, is to let Him.

 **A Timely Tip**

If you're not sure what to do, ask your parents. And pray about your choices. God will always guide you if you let Him. Let Him.

136
Making Better Decisions

Don't turn your back on wisdom, for she will protect you.
Love her, and she will guard you.

PROVERBS 4:6 NLT

Choices. You make a lot of them every day. The more you learn about God's Word—and the more carefully you listen to your parents and your teachers—the better choices you'll make.

The Bible is filled with verses and stories that can teach you how to live wisely and well. God speaks to you through His Word, and if you're smart, you'll listen and learn. When you do, the Lord will help you make wise decisions, which are always better than unwise ones.

 **A Timely Tip**

If you want to make better decisions, slow down and think things through before you decide.

✳ ✳ ✳

137
Celebrating God's Beautiful World

God's glory is on tour in the skies,
God-craft on exhibit across the horizon.

PSALM 19:1 MSG

If you want to think about how great God is, just look up at the stars. He made all the stars you can see plus countless more you can't see. And since God is big enough to create a whole universe out of nothing, you can be sure that He's strong enough to protect you.

Don't take nature for granted. The stars above your head and the ground beneath your feet are part of God's creation. Today and every day, praise the Lord for the amazing things He has made and the incredible things He has done.

✳ ✳ ✳

Today you will encounter God's creation.
When you see the beauty around you,
let each detail remind you to lift your head in praise.

MAX LUCADO

✳ ✳ ✳

138
God Is Always Ready to Help

Since God assured us, "I'll never let you down, never walk off and leave you," we can boldly quote, God is there, ready to help; I'm fearless no matter what. Who or what can get to me?

<small>HEBREWS 13:5–6 MSG</small>

When bad things happen, it's easy to get discouraged. But if you're a Christian, there's no need to stay discouraged for long. Why? Because God has promised to protect you now and forever, that's why.

So the next time you're worried or afraid, remember this: God is with you and He loves you. And whether your problem is a big one or a small one, He can handle it. He is your Shepherd, and He's promised to watch over you today, tomorrow, and throughout all eternity. Just do your best, and let Him do the rest.

✳ ✳ ✳

He is always thinking about us. We are before His eyes. The Lord's eye never sleeps, but is always watching out for our welfare. We are continually on His heart.

<small>C. H. SPURGEON</small>

*** *** ***

139
It Pays to Use Your Time Wisely

We must do the works of Him who sent Me while it is day.
Night is coming when no one can work.

JOHN 9:4 HCSB

It's easy to waste time. And it's easy to put off important things until later so you can do unimportant things now. But God wants you to use your time wisely, and that's what you should want for yourself.

When you think about it, you've got lots of ways to spend your time. You can do important things, like schoolwork or reading God's Word, or you can spend most of your day in front of a screen watching shows or playing games. Whenever you decide to do the important work first, you've made a wise choice.

The Lord has big plans for you and important work He wants you to do. And when you use your time wisely, He'll bless your work today and always.

*** *** ***

Time is a precious gift, because you only have a set amount of it.

RICK WARREN

✳ ✳ ✳

140
Be Fair and Honest

The LORD hates dishonest scales,
but he is pleased with honest weights.

PROVERBS 11:1 NCV

God wants us to deal fairly with our families, with our friends, with our neighbors, and even with complete strangers. And the Lord warns us that dishonest behavior will be punished. So, it's always better to be honest.

When you make a habit of telling the truth every time, you'll stay out of trouble, and your friends will respect you for it. So always tell the truth, the whole truth, and nothing but the truth. You'll be glad you did…and God will be glad, too.

☞ Remember This

When you play fairly, other kids notice. And they'll appreciate your honesty. It's better to play fairly and lose than to cheat and win.

✳ ✳ ✳

141
Got Questions?

If you need wisdom, ask our generous God,
and he will give it to you. He will not rebuke you for asking.

JAMES 1:5 NLT

When you have a question, what do you do? If you're in class, do you raise your hand? If you're at home, do you ask your parents? If you're not sure about something, do you ask somebody who knows? Hopefully, the answer to all these questions is yes. When you have a question, you shouldn't be afraid to ask it.

The Bible has answers, too. And you can be sure that God's promises never fail and His wisdom never grows old.

So if you need to know something, ask. Ask your parents, ask your teachers, and ask your heavenly Father. They want to hear your questions, and they have all the answers you need.

✳ ✳ ✳

God has never turned away the questions of a sincere searcher.

MAX LUCADO

✳ ✳ ✳

142
Enough Is Enough

Keep your lives free from the love of money,
and be satisfied with what you have.

HEBREWS 13:5 NCV

*A*re you satisfied with the things you have, or are you always trying to get more? If you focus too much on the stuff you own, you won't have the time or energy to focus on the really important things in life.

God wants you to be a good person and a humble servant. He wants you to obey His rules and follow His Son. The Lord doesn't particularly care about the kind of clothes you wear or the kind of car your parents drive. God cares about you, not your possessions. So the next time you're tempted to spend your last dime on something that's not very important, slow down, take a deep breath, and ask yourself if you really need more stuff. Maybe you do. But, it's more likely that you don't.

✳ ✳ ✳

Contentment is possible when we stop striving for more.

CHARLES SWINDOLL

✳ ✳ ✳
143
Be Thankful Now!

And whatever you do, in word or in deed,
do everything in the name of the Lord Jesus,
giving thanks to God the Father through Him.

COLOSSIANS 3:17 HCSB

*A*re you a grateful person? You should be. After all, you've got plenty of things to be thankful for. Even on those days when you're sad, or angry, or tired, you're still a very lucky person.

Who has given you all the blessings you enjoy? Your parents are responsible, of course. But all of our blessings really start with God. That's why we should thank Him many times each day.

The Lord has given you so much—more blessings than you can count—so thank Him now...and don't ever stop.

 A Timely Tip

It's always a good time to thank God for His gifts. In fact, you can thank Him many times each day...and you should.

144
God Is Strong Enough
to Take Care of Any Problem

Don't fret or worry. Instead of worrying, pray. Let petitions and praises shape your worries into prayers, letting God know your concerns. Before you know it, a sense of God's wholeness, everything coming together for good, will come and settle you down. It's wonderful what happens when Christ displaces worry at the center of your life.

PHILIPPIANS 4:6–7 MSG

If you have a problem, what should you do? You should talk to your parents and there's something else you can do: you can pray about it.

If there is something you're worried about, you should ask God to give you comfort. If there is a person you don't like, you should pray for a forgiving heart. And as you pray more, you'll discover that God is always near and that He's always ready to hear from you. So don't worry about things; pray about them. God is waiting to hear from you, and He's ready to listen now.

✳ ✳ ✳

God is bigger than your problems. Whatever worries press upon you today, put them in God's hands and leave them there.

BILLY GRAHAM

✳ ✳ ✳
145
Loving God, Loving People

Jesus answered, "'Love the Lord your God with all your heart, all your soul, and all your mind.' This is the first and most important command. And the second command is like the first: 'Love your neighbor as you love yourself.'"

MATTHEW 22:37–39 NCV

When He was asked to name God's most important commandments, Jesus said that we should love the Lord (first) and love our neighbors (second). For Christ, these were the two most important rules in the Bible. And if these rules were good enough for Him, they should be good enough for us, too.

When you love God—and when you show Him that you love Him by obeying His commandments—you'll be blessed. And when you treat other people as you want to be treated, you'll be blessed yet again. So please don't delay. Love God and your neighbors today.

☞ Remember This

God's greatest commandment is easy to understand. He wants you to love Him, and He wants you to be kind to other people.

146
You'll Be Rewarded
When You Obey the Rules

Do you want to be counted wise, to build a reputation for wisdom? Here's what you do: Live well, live wisely, live humbly. It's the way you live, not the way you talk, that counts.

JAMES 3:13 MSG

The Bible promises that good behavior is rewarded and bad behavior isn't. But some people misbehave anyway. Please don't behave like that.

When your teachers or parents aren't watching, what should you do? The answer, of course, is that you should behave exactly as you would if they were watching you. Even when no grown-ups are around, it's up to you to be a good person and be a good Christian.

Your parents want you to behave; your teachers want you to behave; and so, by the way, does God. The Lord blesses good people—like you—who obey the rules even when the grown-ups aren't watching.

* * *

If you want to reach your potential, you need to add a strong work ethic to your talent.

JOHN MAXWELL

✳ ✳ ✳
147
That Little Voice

Behold, the kingdom of God is within you.

Luke 17:21 KJV

There's a little voice inside your head and your heart. It's called your conscience, and you should listen to it.

God gave you a conscience for a very good reason: to use it. When you do, you'll be glad. But if you ignore your conscience, you'll be sad, and soon.

So the next time you have a feeling that your conscience is trying to tell you something, pay attention. God may be trying to send you a message that you really need to hear.

✳ ✳ ✳

One's conscience can only be satisfied when God is satisfied.

C. H. Spurgeon

* * *

148
Be Humble

But God gives us even more grace, as the Scripture says,
"God is against the proud, but he gives grace to the humble."

JAMES 4:6 NCV

The Bible teaches us to be humble, but for some of us, it's a hard lesson to learn. In our weaker moments, we're tempted to brag about the things we've done. But the Lord knows that all our blessings begin with Him. So He instructs us to be humble, not prideful.

The good things in our lives, including our loved ones, come from God. He deserves the credit, not us. And we deserve the experience of praising Him for His blessings.

So today, as you think about the things you've done and the victories you've won, stay humble. Praise the Lord above, not the boy you see when you look in the mirror.

* * *

Do you wish to be great? Then begin by being humble.

ST. AUGUSTINE

*** ✳ ✳ ✳

149
Be on Guard against Evil

Because the eyes of the Lord are on the righteous
and His ears are open to their request.
But the face of the Lord is against those who do evil.

1 PETER 3:12 HCSB

Sometimes people behave badly. Maybe they say cruel things, or maybe they try to hurt your friends. When people misbehave, you can be sure that God is watching. And He'll decide how and when to punish the people who have disobeyed Him.

When mean people are unkind to you—or unkind to someone you like—you may be tempted to strike back in anger. Please resist that temptation! Instead, remember that God sees all things and corrects all problems in His own way. Your job is to protect yourself, to forgive as quickly as you can, and move on.

☛ Remember This

There are many ways to get into trouble. So you should be on the lookout for problems before they arrive—and try to figure out ways to avoid them—before little problems turn into big ones.

* * *

50
Do the Right Thing

For the Kingdom of God is not just a lot of talk;
it is living by God's power.

1 CORINTHIANS 4:20 NLT

Everybody makes mistakes, and you'll make some, too. It's not always easy to do the right thing, especially when you're frustrated or tired. But doing the wrong thing almost always leads to trouble. And sometimes it can ead to BIG trouble.

When you follow your conscience and do the right thing, you don't have to worry about what you did or what you said. But if you are dishonest—or if you do something that you know is wrong—you'll be worried that other people will find out. So do the right thing; it may be harder in the beginning, but it's always easier in the end.

* * *

Life is a series of choices between the bad, the good,
and the best. Everything depends on how we choose.

VANCE HAVNER

153

151
Trust God's Love

*But God proves His own love for us in that
while we were still sinners, Christ died for us!*

ROMANS 5:8 HCSB

If God had a refrigerator in heaven, your picture would be on it. That fact should make you feel very good about the person you are and the person you can become.

God's love for you is bigger and more wonderful than you can imagine. He loves you so much that He sent His Son to this earth so that you can have eternal life.

It's up to you to accept God's love and welcome His Son Jesus into your heart. When you do, you'll feel better about yourself, and your life will be changed forever. So don't delay; trust God's love—and His Son—today.

✳ ✳ ✳

*A man's spiritual health is exactly proportional
to his love for God.*

C. S. LEWIS

152
God Wants You
to Have a Great Life

*I have come so that they may have life
and have it in abundance.*

JOHN 10:10 HSCB

God wants to bless you in many ways. He has big plans for you, plans for life here on earth and for an amazing life in heaven. But God probably won't give you everything you want, at least not at first. He expects you to do your part of the work that's required to make His plans come true. That means that you'll need to become the kind of person that the Lord—and your parents—want you to be. So remember this: You have a very bright future. To achieve your dreams, you'll need to behave yourself and obey the Lord. When you do, good things will happen...many good things.

✳ ✳ ✳

*God loves you and wants you to experience
peace and life—abundant and eternal.*

BILLY GRAHAM

153
The Rule That's Golden

Here is a simple, rule-of-thumb for behavior:
Ask yourself what you want people to do for you,
then grab the initiative and do it for them.
Add up God's Law and Prophets and this is what you get.

MATTHEW 7:12 MSG

How should we treat other people? Jesus has the answer to that question. He wants us to treat others exactly like we want to be treated ourselves. It's the Golden Rule, and it should be your rule, too. When you use the Golden Rule as your guide for living, your words and your actions will be pleasing to other people and to God.

So, if you want to know how to treat other people, ask the person you see every time you look into the mirror. The answer you receive will tell you exactly what to do.

Do all the good you can. By all the means you can. In all the ways you can. In all the places you can. At all the times you can. To all the people you can. As long as ever you can.

JOHN WESLEY

✳ ✳ ✳

154
He's Listening

One day Jesus told his disciples a story to show that
they should always pray and never give up.

LUKE 18:1 NLT

Jesus told His disciples that they should pray always. And so should you. Genuine, heartfelt prayer changes things and it changes you. When you talk to your Father in heaven, you're connecting with a never-ending source of divine wisdom and infinite love.

Do you have questions that you simply can't answer? Ask for the Lord's guidance. Do you want to receive the gift of everlasting love and eternal life? Accept the grace of God's only begotten Son. Whatever your need, no matter how great or small, pray about it. Instead of waiting for mealtimes or bedtimes, follow the instruction of your Savior: pray always and never lose heart. And remember: God is not just near; He is here, and He's ready to talk with you. Now!

✳ ✳ ✳

If something is important to you, it's important to God.
Does God care about the little things in our lives?
You better believe it. If it matters to you, it matters to Him.

MAX LUCADO

✳ ✳ ✳
155
Each Day Is a Gift

What joy for those who can live in your house,
always singing your praises. What joy for those
whose strength comes from the LORD....

PSALM 84:4–5 NLT

God wants you to be a joyful person. But that doesn't mean that you'll be happy all the time. Sometimes you may feel upset, or angry, or worried. When you're feeling a little tired or sad, here's something to remember: This day is a gift from God, and it's up to you to enjoy it. So even on those days when things are a little crazy, try your best to be helpful, courteous, and kind. When you share kind words and good deeds, you'll cheer up the people around you. And who knows? You might even cheer yourself up, too.

☞ Remember This

The best day to be happy is this one. You have many reasons to celebrate, so don't delay; let the celebration begin today.

✳ ✳ ✳
156
Pay Attention to God!

Worship the Lord your God and...serve only Him.
MATTHEW 4:10 HCSB

God is everywhere you've ever been and everywhere you'll ever be. But if you're not careful, you may not pay Him much attention. If you're busy, or worried, or sad, or distracted, you may forget that God is always with you, hearing every word you say, knowing every thought you think.

Today and every day, remind yourself that God is near, and that He loves you. That means you're never alone. The Lord is with you now and forever.

☞ Remember This

When you're praying, or when you're in church, try hard to give God your full attention. He deserves it!

157
Don't Be Selfish, Be Generous

Happy are those who think about the poor.
When trouble comes, the LORD will save them.

PSALM 41:1 NCV

Many people aren't as fortunate as you are. These folks don't have enough money to buy the things they really need, so they go without things that you may take for granted. Some of these people live in faraway places, which makes it harder to help them. But lots of needy people live very near you.

Ask your parents to help you find ways to do nice things for people who need your help. And please don't forget that everybody needs love, respect, and kindness, so you should always be ready to share those things, too.

✳ ✳ ✳

Selfishness is as far from Christianity as darkness is from light.

C. H. SPURGEON

⁂ 158
God's Greatest Promise

I assure you: Anyone who believes has eternal life.

JOHN 6:47 HCSB

Now, it's time to remind yourself of a promise that God made a long time ago—the promise that He sent His Son Jesus to save the world and to save you. When you stop to think about it, there can be no greater promise than that.

No matter where you are, God is with you. God loves you, and He sent His Son so that you can live forever in heaven with your loved ones. WOW! That's the greatest promise in the history of the universe. The End.

 A Timely Tip

God offers you the priceless gift of eternal life. If you have not yet accepted His gift, the best moment to do so is now.

＊＊＊
159
Real Friends

Friends come and friends go,
but a true friend sticks by you like family.

Proverbs 18:24 MSG

The book of Proverbs teaches us that true friends are as loyal as family members. How wonderful it is to have real friends we can trust. So we should thank God for the friends He has brought into our lives because these people are, indeed, gifts from above.

Today and every day, we should thank God for the gift of friendship. It's a beautiful gift that can last a lifetime.

 **A Timely Tip**

The best rule for making and keeping friends is, not surprisingly, the Golden one. To have good friends, be a good friend.

* * *

160
How to Treat Your Neighbors

The whole law is made complete in this one command:
"Love your neighbor as you love yourself."

GALATIANS 5:14 NCV

How should you treat your neighbors? The Bible says that you should treat them in exactly the same way you'd want to be treated if you were in their shoes.

Do you want to be the best person you can be? Then invite Christ to rule over your heart and then share His love with your family, with your friends, and with your neighbors. They'll be glad you did, and you'll be glad, too.

* * *

If my heart is right with God,
every human being is my neighbor.

OSWALD CHAMBERS

* * *

161
You Should Read the Book That God Wrote

For I am not ashamed of the gospel, because it is God's power for salvation to everyone who believes.

Romans 1:16 HCSB

If you want to know more about God, you should read the book He wrote. So, how often do you pick up your Bible? The Bible is not like any other book. It is an amazing gift from the Lord, and it contains promises you can trust.

God's holy Word is a life-changing, one-of-a-kind treasure. Please handle it with care, but more importantly, handle it every day!

 **A Timely Tip**

The more you use your Bible, the more God will use you.

162
Sooner or Later, the Truth Comes Out!

The honest person will live in safety,
but the dishonest will be caught.

PROVERBS 10:9 NCV

Sometimes telling the truth can be hard, but you should always tell the truth, even when you'd rather not. If you say something that isn't true, people will usually figure out that you've told a lie. Then, you'll *really* be sorry.

If you're afraid to tell the truth, ask God to give you the courage to do the right thing. With God's help, you can be honest and stay out of trouble.

If you've ever told a big lie and had to live with the consequences, you know that it's far more trouble—and much more complicated—to tell a lie than it is to tell the truth. But lies aren't just troubling to us; they're also troubling to God. So do yourself a favor: be honest, even when it's hard. You'll be glad you did, and God will be glad, too.

 A Timely Tip

Since the truth always comes out eventually, you might as well go ahead and tell the truth the first time. It will save you lots of headaches and heartaches.

✳ ✳ ✳

163
Be Satisfied

Your life should be free from the love of money.
Be satisfied with what you have, for He Himself has said,
I will never leave you or forsake you.

HEBREWS 13:5 HCSB

Where can you find contentment? Is it the result of being rich or famous, or both? Nope. Genuine contentment is a gift from God to those who trust Him and follow His commandments. You can't buy happiness in a store, and you can't purchase peace of mind, either. So don't even try.

Today and every day, seek God first and welcome His Son into your heart. When you do, you'll find contentment, and it won't cost you a penny.

 **A Timely Tip**

If you want to be happy, remember that the things you own aren't nearly as important as the person you become.

* * *
164
Teamwork Works!

A kingdom that is divided cannot continue,
and a family that is divided cannot continue.

MARK 3:24–25 NCV

No matter where you are or what you're doing, it pays to be a good teammate. Teamwork works at home, at school, and just about every place in between.

Cooperation begins with sharing: sharing your enthusiasm, sharing your encouragement, sharing your dreams, and sharing the stage. So if you want to be a real winner in the game of life, make sure that you're always willing to work with your teammates. When you and your friends work together, great things can happen.

☞ Remember This

Teamwork works. Selfishness doesn't.

165
Look before You Leap

Enthusiasm without knowledge is no good;
haste makes mistakes.

PROVERBS 19:2 NLT

Do you always look before you leap? If so, congratulations. But if you sometimes leap first and look second, God wants to have a little talk with you.

The Bible teaches us that we should behave wisely, not carelessly. But sometimes we're tempted to rush ahead and do things before we think about them. Sometimes, because of our haste, we make needless mistakes.

If you're one of those boys who does things in a hurry and often regrets it, do yourself a big favor—slow down, think things through, and look carefully before you leap. It's the safe way—and the wise way—to behave.

 **A Timely Tip**

Sometimes being wise is nothing more than slowing down long enough to think about things before you do them.

* * *

166
Avoiding Arguments

Foolish people are always fighting,
but avoiding quarrels will bring you honor.

PROVERBS 20:3 NCV

Some people always seem to be getting themselves into arguments. Hopefully, you're not one of those people.

The Bible teaches us that it's better to walk away from an argument than to start one. And that's good advice whether you're at home, at school, or just about anywhere in between.

The less you argue, the better you'll feel about yourself, your friends, and your world. So here's some advice, straight from God's Word: don't start arguments, and when you happen upon one, don't join in.

 **A Timely Tip**

Arguments usually cause many more problems than they solve. So don't be afraid to leave the scene of an argument.

*** *** ***

167
Wisdom and Guidance
from Above

*The LORD says, "I will make you wise and show you
where to go. I will guide you and watch over you."*

PSALM 32:8 NCV

If you want to become smarter and wiser, here are some things you should do. First, you should listen carefully to your parents. You should pay attention to your teachers. And you should spend time learning about the things God wants you to do.

The Bible is filled with promises that you can trust. The Lord will guide you if you pay attention to His instructions and welcome His Son into your heart. When you obey God and follow His Son, you will be rewarded now and forever. So guard your heart and trust your heavenly Father. He will never lead you astray.

*** *** ***

*The beautiful thing about this adventure called faith
is that we can count on God never to lead us astray.*

CHARLES SWINDOLL

✳ ✳ ✳
168
God Wants You in His Church

If two or three people come together in my name,
I am there with them.

MATTHEW 18:20 NCV

God wants you to be an active member of His church. Why? Because He knows that church is the right place for you, and He wants you to be happy, healthy, and wise.

When you go to church, be sure to pay attention and be sure to behave yourself. Try to learn as much as you can, and try to help as many people as you can.

If you have the right attitude, church can be a fabulous, fun place to hear God's message. So make sure your attitude is right, and then go to church with a happy heart. Your heavenly Father wants you there...and Father knows best.

✳ ✳ ✳

Only participation in the full life
of a local church builds spiritual muscle.

RICK WARREN

※ ※ ※

169
God Wants You to Behave Yourself

A good person produces good deeds and words season after season.
MATTHEW 12:35 MSG

God wants you to make good choices. He wants you to behave yourself. And He wants you to be kind and generous. But sometimes you may be tempted to pay less attention to the things God wants and more attention to the things your friends want. That's when you should remember that pleasing God is far more important than pleasing other people.

Even when nobody's watching, God is. And He knows whether you've done the right thing or the wrong thing. So if you're tempted to misbehave when nobody is looking, remember this: There is never a time when "nobody's watching." Somebody is always watching over you— and that Somebody, of course, is your Father in heaven. Don't let Him down!

☞ Remember This

There is never a time when nobody is watching. God is always watching! Even when nobody else is around, God is with you.

* * *

170
Be Like Barnabas

*Now Joseph, a Levite of Cyprian birth,
who was also called Barnabas by the apostles
(which translated means Son of Encouragement)...*

ACTS 4:36 NASB

Barnabas was a man who became a leader in the early Christian church. He was known for his kindness and for his ability to encourage others. Barnabas made other people feel good about themselves. And, because of him, many people were introduced to Christ.

We become like Barnabas when we speak kind words to our friends and family members. When we are helpful and kind, the people around us can see how Christians should behave. So today and every day, be an encouraging friend, just like Barnabas.

☞ Remember This

God wants you to be helpful, kind, and courteous. And He wants you to help other people whenever you can.

171

Distractions and Temptations

Stay alert! Watch out for your great enemy, the devil.
He prowls around like a roaring lion, looking for someone to devour.
Stand firm against him, and be strong in your faith.

1 PETER 5:8–9 NLT

Whether you realize it or not, you're surrounded by things that can waste your time and your energy. These things are called "distractions," and they tempt you to spend many hours focusing on unimportant things and zero hours focusing on the things that can make you a better person and a better Christian.

When you're tempted to spend countless hours in front of a big screen—or a small one—remember that God has important things He wants you to do. And if you're tempted to misbehave, remember that God has rules, and your parents have rules, too.

When you learn to avoid distractions and temptations, you'll be surprised at what you can do with all the time you saved. And you'll be pleased with the results.

✳ ✳ ✳

Our Lord has given us an example of how to overcome the
devil's temptations. When He was tempted in the wilderness,
He defeated Satan every time by the use of the Bible.

BILLY GRAHAM

172
Choose Wisely

I am offering you life or death, blessings or curses.
Now, choose life!... To choose life is to love the LORD your God,
obey him, and stay close to him.

DEUTERONOMY 30:19–20 NCV

God gave Adan and Eve all the things they needed to live happily-ever-after in a beautiful place called the Garden of Eden. But the Lord warned them not to eat the fruit of a particular tree. So what did Adam and Eve do? You probably know the story: They disobeyed God and ate the fruit anyway! It was a very big mistake that led to lots of trouble.

Like Adam and Eve, God gives each of us the ability to make our own choices. When we choose wisely, we are blessed. But when we make unwise choices, we must face the consequences.

Today and every day, you have many choices to make. Please choose wisely—and expect to receive God's blessings when you do.

✳ ✳ ✳

You have to say "yes" to God first before you can
effectively say "no" to the devil

VANCE HAVNER

✳ ✳ ✳
173
It's Important to Be Honest

Good people will be guided by honesty;
dishonesty will destroy those who are not trustworthy.

PROVERBS 11:3 NCV

The Bible says that it's important to be honest. And your parents say the same thing. So do your grandparents, your teachers, your coaches, and your pastor. So the old saying must be true: "Honesty is the best policy."

When you tell the truth, you'll feel better about yourself, and other people will feel better about you, too. But that's not all. When you tell the truth, God knows—and He will reward you for your honesty.

Telling the truth is hard sometimes. But it's better to be honest, even when it's hard. So remember this: telling the truth is always the right thing to do...always.

☞ Remember This

Honesty pays. Dishonesty costs. Behave accordingly.

✳ ✳ ✳
174
You Can Learn a Lot from Ants

Go watch the ants, you lazy person. Watch what they do and be wise. Ants have no commander, no leader or ruler, but they store up food in the summer and gather their supplies at harvest.

Proverbs 6:6–8 NCV

The Bible teaches us that we can learn an important lesson from a surprising source: ants. Ants are hard-working little creatures. They do their work without being told what to do. They work hard all day. When they're not sleeping, they're doing their jobs. And as far as we know, they never complain. We should do likewise.

The Lord has big plans for you, plans that will probably require some hard work along the way. And that's okay with God because He knows you can do it. With the Lord's help, you can make your dreams come true *if* you're willing to work for them. The rest is up to you.

✳ ✳ ✳

We must trust as if it all depended on God and work as if it all depended on us.

C. H. Spurgeon

* * *

175
Don't Be Stingy

Remember: A stingy planter gets a stingy crop;
a lavish planter gets a lavish crop.

2 CORINTHIANS 9:6 MSG

Sometimes you may not feel like sharing. You may be tempted to keep everything for yourself. But God has other plans. He wants you to share with people who have less than you. So if you want to please the Lord, you can't be stingy; you must be generous and kind.

Sometime soon—maybe even today—you'll have a chance to help somebody. Maybe you'll even have an opportunity to give something away. When it happens, remember what God wants you to do. Be generous to others, just as the Lord has been generous to you.

* * *

Abundant living means abundant giving.

E. STANLEY JONES

✳ ✳ ✳

176
Jesus Is Your Friend

I am the good shepherd. The good shepherd
gives His life for the sheep.

John 10:11 NKJV

When you invite Jesus to become your friend, He will do it. He'll be your friend today, tomorrow, and forever. If you make mistakes, He'll stand by you. If you have doubts or fears, He will understand. If you misbehave, He'll still love you. And if you feel sad or sorry, He can help you feel better.

Yes, Jesus loves you more than you know. Accept His love today and share it with your friends, with your family, and with the world. When you tell people about Jesus, you'll show everybody how much He means to you.

If you come to Christ, you will always have the option of an
ever-present friend. He'll be with you every step of the way.

Bill Hybels

177
He Teaches His Ways

Teach me, O LORD, the way of Your statutes,
and I shall keep it to the end.

PSALM 119:33 NKJV

God has many things He wants to teach you. He's included these lessons in a book that's like no other: the Holy Bible. You can trust every word you find in your Bible because every word comes from the Lord. And God always keeps His promises.

When you trust your heavenly Father, He will guide you; He will protect you; and He will bless you. So trust Him. And then get ready for the good things that are sure to come, now and forever.

God is God. He knows what He is doing.

MAX LUCADO

178
Use Time Wisely

Teach us to number our days carefully
so that we may develop wisdom in our hearts.

PSALM 90:12 HCSB

God knows that each day is a gift from above, and He wants us to use His gifts wisely. The Lord wants us to spend our time in ways that are pleasing to Him, and He wants us to avoid silly, time-wasting distractions. But there's a problem. In the world today, we have so many games to play and so many screens to watch, we don't have any time left for more important things.

Even though you're still young, you have important things to do—things like your daily devotional, your schoolwork, and your family time. You should do these things before you start playing games or watching TV, not after. When you do first things first, you'll earn more rewards from life. And you'll feel better about yourself because you'll know that God and your parents are pleased with you, too.

👉 Remember This

If you can't seem to find time for God, then you're simply too busy for your own good. God is never too busy for you, and you should never be too busy for Him.

✳ ✳ ✳

179
Anything Is Possible

But Jesus looked at them and said, "With men
this is impossible, but with God all things are possible."

MATTHEW 19:26 HCSB

With God, anything is possible. If you've got a problem, He can help you solve it. If you have a dream, He can help you achieve it. If you ask for His help or His guidance, He will give it. He never leaves you for a moment, and His love for you never ends.

Throughout history the Lord has worked countless miracles, and He's still doing it today. His miracles come in a variety of shapes and sizes, so keep your eyes and your heart open. Be watchful, and you'll soon be amazed at the wonderful things that God can do.

There is no limit to God. There is no limit to His power.
There is no limit to His love. There is no limit to His mercy.

BILLY GRAHAM

✳ ✳ ✳
180
God Knows the Heart

But I, the Lord, look into a person's heart and test the mind.

JEREMIAH 17:10 NCV

God never leaves us, not even for a moment. Even when nobody else is watching, He is. Nothing that we say or do escapes the watchful eye of our Lord.

God wants you to live according to His rules, not your own. So, the next time that you're tempted to break the rules—or the next time you're tempted to say or do something wrong—remember that you can't keep secrets from God. So don't even try!

☞ Remember This

When nobody else is around, God is. Act accordingly.

***

181
You Can Trust God's Promises

The ways of God are without fault. The LORD's words
are pure. He is a shield to those who trust him.

PSALM 18:30 NCV

God has made quite a few promises to you, and you can be sure that He will keep every single one of them. These promises are found in a book like no other: the Holy Bible.

God's promises never fail and they never grow old. That means you can always trust the things that God says, and you can share His promises with your family, with your friends, and with the world.

Everything you read in the Bible is true, so you can rely on God today, tomorrow, and forever. And *that's* a promise you can depend on.

***

The Bible is God's book of promises, and unlike
the books of man, it does not change or go out of date.

BILLY GRAHAM

* * *

182
Be a Humble Giver

Be careful not to practice your in front of others
to be seen by them. If you do, you will have
no reward from your Father in heaven.

MATTHEW 6:1 NIV

When you give something away, do you make a big announcement? Do you tell everybody how generous you are and try to gain the approval of your family and friends? If so, God wants to have a little chat with you.

The Lord wants us to share our things, but He doesn't want us to make a big deal about it. He wants us to be humble, not proud. God knows that all blessings—including the ones we happen to own—are gifts from Him. That means we should be praising Him, not ourselves.

So the next time you give something away, try to keep it to yourself. It's the best way to give and the best way to live.

 **A Timely Tip**

Don't be afraid to share what you have with others; after all, it all belongs to God anyway.

* * *

183
Today's Happiness

Joyful are those...whose hope is in the Lord *their God.*
PSALM 146:5 NLT

This day is a gift from the Lord. And it's wonderful to celebrate life. But sometimes we don't feel much like celebrating.

If we could decide to be happy "once and for all," life would be so much simpler, but it doesn't seem to work that way. If we want happiness to last, we need to keep creating good thoughts day after day. Yesterday's good thoughts aren't enough; we've got to keep thinking good thoughts *today*.

So make this day a celebration by giving thanks to the Lord. His love for you lasts forever. Accept it joyfully and be happy. Now.

☞ Remember This

If you want to be happy, obey God and celebrate His blessings. If you want to make yourself unhappy, disobey Him and ignore His blessings. And just in case you're wondering, it's better to be happy.

❋ ❋ ❋

184
The Search for Wisdom

But wisdom will help you be good and do what is right.

PROVERBS 2:20 NCV

If you look in a dictionary, you'll see that the word wisdom means "using good judgment, and knowing what is true." But if you want to be very wise, you can't just know what to do; you must also do it. It's not enough to know what's right; you must also do what's right.

Once you've learned something, the Lord wants you to share it. And the best way to share your wisdom—perhaps the only way—is not by your words but by your example. As the old saying goes, "Actions speak louder than words."

❋ ❋ ❋

Mark it down. God never turns away the honest seeker.
Go to God with your questions. You may not find all
the answers, but in finding God, you know the One who does.

MAX LUCADO

185
If You Love Jesus, Tell Somebody

All those who stand before others and say they believe in me,
I will say before my Father in heaven that they belong to me.

MATTHEW 10:32 NCV

Jesus loves you. Do you love Him? If you do—and you certainly should—please tell somebody.

God doesn't want you to be a silent believer; He wants you to share His Good News with your family, with your friends, and with the world. So the next time you get a chance to tell somebody about Jesus, speak up. You'll be doing the other person a huge favor, and you'll be doing the will of God. There's no doubt about it: it's good to talk about your faith.

✳ ✳ ✳

Remember, a small light will do a great deal when it is in
a very dark place. Put one little tallow candle in the middle
of a large hall, and it will give a great deal of light.

D. L. MOODY

❋ ❋ ❋
186
The Person in the Mirror

*You made them only a little lower than God
and crowned them with glory and honor.*

PSALM 8:5 NLT

The boy you see in the mirror is a very special person. The Lord knows that you're special person, and your family knows it, too. There's nobody else in the world like you. In fact, there's nobody else in the whole universe like you.

Because you're so special, and because you're loved by God, you have every reason to be happy about your world, your future, and yourself. God has wonderful plans for you, and He's promised to lead you along the best path for you.

So pray often, behave yourself, and give thanks to the Lord for the special gifts He has given you. And be sure to use those gifts today and every day.

 **A Timely Tip**

Don't ever forget that you are a special creation made by God. He created you and He loves you, now and forever.

187
If You Think You Can

The LORD is my light and my salvation—
so why should I be afraid? The LORD is my fortress,
protecting me from danger—so why should I tremble?

PSALM 27:1 NLT

If you think you can do something, then you can probably do it. If you think you can't do something, then you probably won't do it. So remember this: If you're having a little trouble getting something done, don't get frustrated, don't get discouraged, and don't give up. Just keep trying, and believe in yourself.

When you try hard—and keep trying hard—you'll be surprised at the things you can do. But if you quit at the first sign of trouble, you'll never know what you might have accomplished if you'd kept trying. So here's some simple advice: When you need to finish something, finish it sooner rather than later. It's the best way to work and the best way to live.

✳ ✳ ✳

We don't give up. We look up. We trust. We believe.

MAX LUCADO

✳ ✳ ✳
188
Slow Down and Think

Wise people's minds tell them what to say,
and that helps them be better teachers.

PROVERBS 16:23 NCV

Sometimes it's tempting to make quick decisions. Something grabs our attention, and we react, often without thinking. And that's when it's easy to make a mistake.

The Bible teaches us that it's better to be safe than sorry, which means that we should stop and think before we rush into situations that we don't fully understand.

So, the next time you're tempted to look before you leap, slow down and think about the consequences of your actions. When you take your time, you'll make better decisions, and you'll make safer decisions, too.

 A Timely Tip

Sometimes the smartest thing you can do is to slow down and think before you act. When you take time to think and pray, you'll probably make smarter choices.

✳✳✳

189
Make the Most of Your Talents

Do not neglect the gift that is in you.

1 TIMOTHY 4:14 NKJV

How can you make the most of the talents God has given you? First, you must figure out what you're really good at. Then, you must decide where God is leading you. And finally, you must find the determination to keep improving your skills and developing your talents.

You'll have many opportunities to accomplish great things for the Lord, but you should not expect the work to be easy. So pray as if everything depended upon God, but work as if everything depended upon you. When you do, you can be sure that the Lord will use your talents to make His world—and your world—a better place.

You are the only person on earth who can use your ability.

ZIG ZIGLAR

190
Let Your Words Be Kind

When you talk, do not say harmful things, but say what people need—words that will help others become stronger. Then what you say will do good to those who listen to you.

EPHESIANS 4:29 NCV

If you say nice things and speak kind words, you make other people feel better. And that's exactly what you should do.

How hard is it to say a kind word? Not very! But sometimes we're so busy that we may forget to say something that might make another person feel better. At times like these, God wants us to slow down long enough to be helpful and kind.

Kind words can help; cruel words can hurt. When you say the right thing at the right time, you give a gift that can change somebody's day or somebody's life. So use your words—and choose your words—carefully...*very* carefully.

* * *

Fill the heart with the love of Christ so that only truth and purity can come out of the mouth.

WARREN WIERSBE

* * *

191
The Right Path

Put your hope in the LORD.
Travel steadily along his path. He will honor you....

PSALM 37:34 NLT

God has a plan for your life, and He wants you to stay on the right path: His path. But the world will tempt you to take a very different path. The world is filled with distractions and countless opportunities to disobey God's instructions. But God wants you to stay focused on His rules and His promises. When you do, you'll be happier; you'll be healthier; and you'll be protected.

So the next time you're about to get sidetracked by silly distractions or serious temptations, remember that God has a better plan and a better path. If you're wise, you'll choose God's path every time.

☞ Remember This

It's simple to stay on the right path. Just obey God and follow in the footsteps of His Son.

✳ ✳ ✳

192
Be Kind to Everyone

Let everyone see that you are gentle and kind.
The Lord is coming soon.

PHILIPPIANS 4:5 NCV

Who should you be kind to? Your family? Yes. Your friends? Absolutely. But it doesn't stop there. God wants you to be kind to everybody you meet. And He wants everybody to know you're a Christian by the way you treat other people.

An attitude of kindness starts in your heart and works its way out from there. So put the love of God in your heart and then share it. When you do, you'll make everybody happier. And that includes you.

☞ Remember This

The Golden Rule starts with you, so be kind to your family and friends. And be sure to treat them in the same way that you like to be treated.

✳ ✳ ✳

193
You Need Habits
That Are Pleasing to God

I, the Lord, examine the mind,
I test the heart to give to each according to his way,
according to what his actions deserve.

JEREMIAH 17:10 HCSB

Most kids have a few habits they'd like to change, and maybe you do, too. If so, God wants to help.

If you trust the Lord, and if you keep asking Him to help you change bad habits, He will help you learn to make better choices. And He will help you get rid of those pesky bad habits. So, if at first you don't succeed, keep praying. God is listening, and He's ready to help you become a better person if you ask Him...so ask Him!

 A Timely Tip

First you make your habits, and then your habits make you. So it's always a good time to think about the habits you should make and the ones you should probably break.

* * *

194
Safety Matters

The prudent see danger and take refuge,
but the simple keep going and pay the penalty.

PROVERBS 27:12 NIV

Your safety matters to God; it matters to your parents; and it should matter to you, too.

Self-control and safety go hand in hand. Why? Because a big part of self-control is looking around and thinking things through before you do something that you might regret later.

Have you heard the old saying "Look before you leap!"? Well, if you want to live safely and happily, you should look very carefully before you decide whether or not to leap. After all, it's easy to leap, but once you're in the middle of your jump, it's too late to leap back!

☞ Remember This

If you don't look before you leap, you may start having regrets even before you land.

✳ ✳ ✳

195
Play Fairly

*There is joy for those who deal justly with others
and always do what is right.*

PSALM 106:3 NLT

When you're playing a game, God wants you to play fairly. He doesn't want you to cheat, and He doesn't want you to bend the rules. But if you're one of those people who *really* likes to win, you may be tempted to break the rules. Please avoid that temptation.

Whether you win or lose a game isn't very important. But the way you play the game is important. If you play fairly, God will cheer you on. But if you cheat, you'll be penalized...one way or another. So please play fairly, or don't play at all.

 **A Timely Tip**

When you play, play fairly. God doesn't care whether you win or lose; He cares how you play the game.

196
Temper Tantrums Don't Work

Bad temper is contagious—don't get infected.

PROVERBS 22:25 MSG

Temper tantrums are silly, and they hurt people. When we lose our tempers, we say things that we shouldn't say, and we do things that we shouldn't do.

The Bible tells us that wise people learn to avoid anger. That's why we should learn to control our tempers before our tempers control us.

Jesus doesn't want you to be angry, and He doesn't want your heart to be troubled. He wants your heart to be filled with love, just like His was...and is! And you should want the same thing, too.

✳ ✳ ✳

We are all fallen creatures and all very hard to live with.

C. S. LEWIS

✳ ✳ ✳

197
Watch Out for Trouble!

Don't copy the behavior and customs of this world, but let God transform you into a new person by changing the way you think. Then you will learn to know God's will for you, which is good and pleasing and perfect..

ROMANS 12:2 NLT

In this world, there are plenty of ways to get into trouble. Every day, you're tempted to waste time and energy by chasing after the wrong things. But God has a better plan: He wants you to be *in* the world but not *of* the world. What, exactly, does that mean? It means that you should focus on God's values, not the world's values.

God doesn't want you to copy the latest action hero or some famous movie star. He wants you to copy Jesus. Of course, you can't be exactly like Him. Jesus was perfect; you are not. But you can *try* to copy Christ by learning His teachings and following His commandments. When you do, you'll be blessed today, tomorrow, and forever.

✳ ✳ ✳

The Lord Jesus Christ is still praying for us. He wants us to be in the world but not of it.

CHARLES STANLEY

✳ ✳ ✳
198
It Pays to Be Patient

May God, who gives this patience and encouragement,
help you live in complete harmony with each other,
as is fitting for followers of Christ Jesus.

ROMANS 15:5 NLT

The Bible tells us that God is love and that if we wish to know Him, we must have love in our hearts. Sometimes, of course, when we're tired, angry, or frustrated, it is very hard to be loving, and it's hard to be patient. Thankfully, frustration and anger are feelings that come and go, but God's love lasts forever.

The Lord instructs us to be kind and patient, not rude or mean. And when we obey Him, we are rewarded with good friendships and happy homes. So remember this: it pays to be patient today and every day.

☞ Remember This

When you learn how to be a more patient person, you'll be a happier person, too.

✳ ✳ ✳

199
God's Guidance Never Fails

The counsel of the LORD stands forever,
the plans of His heart from generation to generation.

PSALM 33:11 NASB

God has promised to teach you and guide you. He is always willing to lead you along a path that follows in the footsteps of His Son. The Lord wants you to keep Jesus in your heart today and every day.

God's guidance never fails. He is always listening, and He's ready to talk to you now. When you pray often and read the Bible every day, God will show you the way you should go. So pray, and listen, and learn.

 **A Timely Tip**

Need direction? Let God be your guide. With Him in the lead, you'll never stay lost for long.

200
Always Try to Please God First

Our only goal is to please God whether we live here or there,
because we must all stand before Christ to be judged.

2 CORINTHIANS 5:9–10 NCV

*A*re you trying to please people or God? Hopefully, you're far more concerned with pleasing your heavenly Father than you are with pleasing your friends. But even if you're a very good person, you may still feel a strong urge to impress your friends.

Today and every day, you will have a choice to make: you can choose to please God first, or you can fall victim to peer pressure. The choice is yours—and so are the consequences. Please choose wisely.

✳ ✳ ✳

You must never sacrifice your relationship with God
for the sake of a relationship with another person.

CHARLES STANLEY

*** *** ***

201
Yes, Jesus Loves You!

No one has greater love than this,
that someone would lay down his life for his friends.

JOHN 15:13 HCSB

The Bible says that Jesus loves you. It's an amazing promise with a very happy ending: Christ has already prepared a place for you in heaven. So how should this Good News make you feel? The fact that Jesus loves you should make you a very happy boy, so happy, in fact, that you try your best to do the things that please Him.

Jesus wants you to love and obey God, and He wants you to be kind to everybody. These are simple instructions from the Son of God. Please take them seriously.

*** *** ***

The love of God is revealed in that
He laid down His life for His enemies.

OSWALD CHAMBERS

✳ ✳ ✳

202
You Don't Have to Be Perfect

The LORD says, "Forget what happened before, and do not
think about the past. Look at the new thing I am going to do.
It is already happening. Don't you see it?
I will make a road in the desert and rivers in the dry land."

ISAIAH 43:18–19 NCV

Nobody's perfect, and that's okay with God. He doesn't expect you to be perfect, and you shouldn't expect yourself to be perfect, either.

Are you one of those people who can't stand to make a mistake? Do you think that you must please everybody all the time? When you make a mess of things, do you become terribly upset? If so, here's some simple advice: don't be too hard on yourself!

Mistakes happen; plans go haywire; and accidents occur when we least expect them. These things happen to everybody. So don't let a single mistake get you down, especially if you've learned something along the way.

✳ ✳ ✳

The happiest people in the world are not those who
have no problems, but the people who have learned
to live with those things that are less than perfect.

JAMES DOBSON

203
Keep Going

Patient endurance is what you need now,
so you will continue to do God's will.
Then you will receive all that he has promised.

HEBREWS 10:36 NLT

When things go wrong, it's easy to give up. But usually it's wrong. So, why are we tempted to give up so quickly? Perhaps it's because we're afraid that we might embarrass ourselves if we tried hard but didn't succeed.

The next time you're tempted to give up at the first sign of trouble, say a prayer and ask God to give you the courage to keep going. God will answer your prayer, and when He does, you'll be amazed at the wonderful things the two of you, working together, can accomplish.

By perseverance the snail reached the ark.

C. H. SPURGEON

204
Hope and Happiness

I will lift up my eyes to the hills—from whence comes my help?
My help comes from the LORD, who made heaven and earth.
PSALM 121:1–2 NKJV

Hope and happiness go together like peanut butter and jelly. When you're hopeful, you're happier. And when you're happier, you tend to be more hopeful.

Are you a happy, hope-filled boy? You should be. After all, you have so many reasons to be grateful. You've got special talents and you're learning how to use them. You have people who love you, and you have a Father in heaven who loves you, too. And the Lord has promised to protect you now and forever. So here's some good advice for you: trust God and never lose hope. It's the right way to think and the best way to live.

👉 Remember This

Because you're a Christian, you have many reasons to be hopeful. God loves you and has promised to lead you. Because He is your Shepherd, you should never lose hope.

205

Try Your Best to Make Other People Feel Better!

*Let us think about each other and help
each other to show love and do good deeds.*

HEBREWS 10:24 NCV

*A*s Christians, we are instructed to say kind things and to help other people. So how can we do it? We can start by celebrating their victories and praising their accomplishments. As the old saying goes, "When someone does something good, applaud—you'll make two people happy."

Life is a team sport, and all of us need occasional pats on the back from our teammates. That's why you should look for the good in other people and praise their good qualities and their hard work. When you do, they'll feel better about themselves, and you'll feel better, too.

👉 Remember This

Encouragement is a wonderful gift. You deserve the experience of giving it and receiving it.

206
It's Always a Good Time to Help Other People

Carry one another's burdens;
in this way you will fulfill the law of Christ.

GALATIANS 6:2 HCSB

When is the best time to help somebody in need? The answer to this question is "as soon as you can."

When people need a helping hand, they usually need it sooner rather than later. So the sooner we offer help, the better.

So, the next time you're trying to decide whether or not to help somebody, ask yourself what Jesus would do if He were in your shoes. The answer to that question will tell you what to do...and when to do it.

* * *

He climbs highest who helps another up.

ZIG ZIGLAR

* * *
207
Keep Reading Your Bible

They are blessed who show mercy to others,
for God will show mercy to them.

<small>MATTHEW 5:7 NCV</small>

Do you think about the Bible a lot...or not? Hopefully you try to pay careful attention to the things you learn from God's Word. After all, the Bible is God's message to you. So, it's not just another book on your shelf; it's a priceless treasure from above.

God has many things He wants to teach you, things you really need to learn. So start learning about the Bible now, and keep learning about it for as long as you live!

 A Timely Tip

You're never too young—or too old—to become a student of God's Word. If you're not already reading your Bible every day, the best time to begin is now.

✳ ✳ ✳

208
Help Keep the Peace in Your Family

The peacemakers will be blessed,
for they will be called sons of God.

MATTHEW 5:9 HCSB

Sometimes it's easiest to become angry with the people we love most. After all, we know that they'll still love us no matter how angry we become. But while it's easy to become angry at home, it's usually wrong.

The next time you're tempted to become angry with a brother, or a sister, or a parent, remember that these are the people who love you more than anybody else. So instead of throwing a temper tantrum or starting a fight, slow down, calm down, and cool off. Because peace is always beautiful, especially when it's peace at your house.

☞ Remember This

If you're lucky enough to be a member of a loving, supportive family, then you owe it to yourself—and to them—to be kind and cooperative today and every day.

***
209
Praise Him

Give thanks to Him and praise His name.
For the Yahweh is good, and His love is eternal;
His faithfulness endures through all generations.

PSALM 100:4–5 HCSB

Do you spend much time praising God? You should. God certainly deserves your praise, and you deserve the experience of praising Him. If you're grateful, you should thank Him and praise Him many times each day.

Today, think about all the wonderful things the Lord has done for you. And every time you notice a gift from above, say a prayer of thanks. God's works are marvelous, His gifts are amazing, and His love endures forever.

***

It is only with gratitude that life becomes rich.

DIETRICH BONHOEFFER

✳ ✳ ✳
210
Let God Teach You

Teach me your ways, O LORD, that I may live according to your truth! Grant me purity of heart, so that I may honor you.
PSALM 86:11 NLT

God has many things He wants to teach us. For starters, He wants us to be kind and patient, not mean or rude. The Bible also tells us that God is love and that if we wish to know Him, we must have love in our hearts.

Sometimes, especially when you're tired, frustrated, or angry, it's hard to hear the things that God is trying to tell us. Thankfully, anger and frustration are feelings that come and go, but God's love lasts forever. So the Lord is always willing to guide you.

Today and every day, take time to talk to God in prayer. He is always listening, and He's always ready to teach you something important. Please listen carefully.

☛ Remember This

You still have lots to learn. So, listen carefully to your parents, to your teachers, and to that quiet voice in your head that tells you the difference between right and wrong. It's called your conscience, and God put it there for a reason: He wants you to use it.

211
Staying Out of Trouble

Don't envy bad people; don't even want to be around them.
All they think about is causing a disturbance;
all they talk about is making trouble.

PROVERBS 24:1–2 MSG

If you'd like to have a good attitude, you should choose friends who have a good attitude, too. Why? Because attitudes are contagious—you catch them from the people who are near you. And if you want to behave yourself, you should choose friends who behave themselves, too. Why? Because if they misbehave, you'll be tempted to misbehave, too.

If your friends say unkind things—or if they misbehave in other ways—it's easy to follow the crowd, even if it's wrong. But the Bible tells us over and over again that we should always do the right thing, not the easy thing. No exceptions.

When your friends misbehave, it can spoil everything. So if your friends behave badly, don't copy them. And if your friends keep behaving badly, choose different friends.

☞ Remember This

You will eventually become more and more like your friends. So be sure to make friends with people who will make you better, not worse.

✳ ✳ ✳

212
Don't Let Your Heart Be Troubled!

Your heart must not be troubled.
Believe in God; believe also in Me.

JOHN 14:1 HCSB

If you're worried about something, talk to your parents. Your parents love you and care for you, and they will protect you. And it's the same way with God. You can talk to Him about your problems, too. When you pray, God will listen. And He's promised to protect you now and forever.

So if you're anxious or afraid, there's always somebody you can talk to. You can talk to your parents, and you can talk to God. So don't keep things to yourself; start talking now.

 A Timely Tip

If you're worried about something, talk to your parents. They want to hear from you, and so does God. So you should pray about your worries, too.

Keep Searching
for the Right Kind of Treasure

Wherever your treasure is,
there the desires of your heart will also be.

<small>LUKE 12:34 NLT</small>

When you turn on the TV, you immediately see messages—advertisements and shows—that try to convince you that material possessions—money and all the things money can buy—are important. But these things aren't important to God, so they shouldn't be very important to you.

The Bible teaches us that we cannot worship both God and stuff at the same time. So you've got an important choice to make: will you put God first in your life, or will you instead worry about collecting stuff, stuff, and more stuff? The answer should be obvious. Please make the right choice.

✳✳✳

You will not be in heaven two seconds before you cry out, why did I place so much importance on things that were so temporary? What was I thinking? Why did I waste so much time, energy and concern on what wasn't going to last?

<small>RICK WARREN</small>

* * *

214
The Size of Your Problems

The righteous person faces many troubles,
but the LORD comes to the rescue each time.

PSALM 34:19 NLT

Nobody's perfect. Everybody makes mistakes, and that includes you. So what do you do when you have a problem? Do you let it ruin your day? Hopefully not.

If something's got you worried, talk to your parents. They can help you understand whether your troubles are really as big as you think they are. And while you're at it, ask your parents to help you figure out what you can do to make things right. Then, get busy fixing the things you can fix…and let God take care of the rest.

☞ Remember This

There are two kinds of problems that you should never worry about: the small ones that you can handle and the big ones that God can handle.

✳ ✳ ✳

215
Two Bible Verses to Memorize

Today, try to memorize these verses from the Bible:

✳ ✳ ✳

*For God so loved the world that He gave
His only begotten Son, that whoever believes in Him
should not perish but have everlasting life.*

JOHN 3:16 NKJV

✳ ✳ ✳

*I have come that they may have life,
and that they may have it more abundantly.*

JOHN 10:10 NKJV

216
If You Make a Mistake, Admit It

If you hide your sins, you will not succeed.
If you confess and reject them, you will receive mercy.

PROVERBS 28:13 NCV

When you make a mistake, what do you do? Do you admit your mistake and apologize to the people you've hurt? Do you try to fix things as soon as possible? And do you learn from your mistake so you won't make it again? Hopefully so.

Everybody makes mistakes, and you will, too. Smart people admit their mistakes and try to make things right. Other people try to hide their mistakes, but the truth usually comes out anyway. So, if you make a mistake, admit it, learn from it, and don't repeat it. It's the right way to behave and the sensible way to live.

 **A Timely Tip**

If you make a mistake, the time to make things better is now, not later! The sooner you admit your mistake, the better.

✳ ✳ ✳
217
Learning from the Right People

Walk with the wise and become wise;
associate with fools and get in trouble.

PROVERBS 13:20 NLT

You have lots to learn. Be sure you're learning from the right people. Your parents and grandparents want to help you grow up to be a wise person and a good Christian. You can always trust them. And you can trust your teachers, too. But sometimes the messages you get from TV (or other kinds of media) aren't the best. So if you're not sure what to watch—or if you're not sure if a particular program is teaching you the right way to behave—talk about it with your parents. They'll tell you which lessons are the good kind and which ones aren't.

✳ ✳ ✳

We urgently need people who encourage
and inspire us to move toward God
and away from the world's enticing pleasures.

JIM CYMBALA

***

218
The Words You Speak
Are Important

Well-spoken words bring satisfaction;
well-done work has its own reward.

PROVERBS 12:14 MSG

The words you choose are very important because they can help people or hurt them. When you are kind and encouraging, you make things better. And that's what God wants you to do.

The Bible reminds us that words are powerful things, so you should use them—and choose them—with care. So today and every day, choose words that are kind and helpful. When you do, your friends will feel better, and you'll feel better, too.

***

Attitude and the spirit in which we communicate
are as important as the words we say.

CHARLES STANLEY

***

219
How Often Should We Forgive?

*Then Peter came to him and asked, "Lord, how often
should I forgive someone who sins against me?
Seven times?" "No, not seven times,"
Jesus replied, "but seventy times seven!"*

MATTHEW 18:21–22 NLT

If you forgive somebody once, that's enough, right? Wrong! Even if you've forgiven somebody many times before, you must keep forgiving.

How often does God forgive us? More times than we can count! And that, by the way, is exactly how many times God expects us to forgive other people—more times than we care to count.

You can be sure that God won't ever get tired of forgiving you. And, because He has forgiven you, He doesn't want you to stop forgiving other people...ever!

👉 Remember This

When it comes to forgiveness, once is not enough. You must continue to forgive. Father's orders!

220
Choosing to Be Obedient

The one who has My commands and keeps them is the one who
loves Me. And the one who loves Me will be loved by
My Father. I also will love him and will reveal Myself to him.

JOHN 14:21 HCSB

You have a choice to make: are you going to be an obedient person or not? The decision to be obedient—or the decision not to be—is a choice you must make for yourself.

Whenever you decide to behave yourself, you're making a wise choice. If you decide to obey your parents, you've made another good decision. If you decide to pay attention to your teachers, you've made yet another wise choice.

So, what kind of person will you choose to be? An obedient, well-behaved person, or the opposite? Before you answer that question, please remember this: obedience pays…and disobedience doesn't.

* * *

You cannot know and do the will of God
without paying the price of obedience.

HENRY BLACKABY

✳ ✳ ✳
221
God Sees Your Heart

Man does not see what the LORD sees, for man sees
what is visible, but the LORD sees the heart.

1 SAMUEL 16:7 HCSB

When people look at you, they only see the outside. But God sees much more than that. He doesn't care how you look on the outside. Why? Because the Lord knows everything about you, and He sees your heart.

If you're like most boys, you'll worry a little bit about the way you look (or maybe you'll worry a lot about it). But please don't worry too much about your appearance! How you look on the outside is not very important, but how you feel on the inside is important. So don't spend too much time trying to impress other people. Instead, try to impress God by being the best person you can be. It's the Lord's opinion that counts.

☞ Remember This

God knows everything about you. He knows your heart, and He loves you. Be thankful for His love and return it.

* * *

222
It's Wise to Behave Yourself

The one who has My commands and keeps them is the one who
loves Me. And the one who loves Me will be loved by
My Father. I also will love him and will reveal Myself to him.

JOHN 14:21 HCSB

Why should you behave yourself? Several reasons. First, it's what God wants. Second, your parents want you to behave well, too. But there's another very good reason to do the right thing: good behavior usually gets noticed, and eventually it gets rewarded.

When you do what's right, you'll please God, you'll please your family, and you'll please most of your friends. But if you misbehave, you'll create problems for yourself and for other people, too. So remember this simple fact: good behavior is rewarded and bad behavior isn't. Then act accordingly. It's the smart thing to do and the wise way to live.

* * *

The Bible teaches that when we turn our backs
on God and choose to disregard His moral laws
there are inevitable consequences.

BILLY GRAHAM

225

*** *

223
Promises You Can Trust

*Let us hold tightly without wavering to the hope
we affirm, for God can be trusted to keep his promise.*

HEBREWS 10:23 NLT

The Bible is filled with stories, advice, and promises. The stories are true, the advice is great, and the promises never fail. When the Lord makes a promise, He keeps it. He's always true to His Word.

When you trust your heavenly Father completely, He will bless you and guide you. And when you invite Jesus into your heart, God will make a special home for you in heaven. Your job is to trust God and obey His commandments. Then, get ready for great things to happen.

☞ Remember This

The Bible is filled with promises, and God will keep every one of them.

224
Fear Not

They won't be afraid of bad news;
*their hearts are steady because they trust the L*ORD.

PSALM 112:7 NCV

Sometimes the world can be a scary place. When you look at the news or hear about bad things happening around the world, you may be worried that bad things are going to happen to you, too.

If you're worried or afraid, talk to the people who love you most. You can talk to parents, grandparents, and people you trust. And you should also talk to the Lord in prayer.

It's okay to be afraid—all of us are fearful from time to time. And it's good to know that you can talk about your fears with loved ones and with God. When you do, you'll soon discover that fear lasts for a little while, but love lasts forever.

✳ ✳ ✳

Meet your fears with faith.

MAX LUCADO

✳ ✳ ✳
225
You Can Do Great Things for God

*I assure you: The one who believes in Me will also
do the works that I do. And he will do even greater works
than these, because I am going to the Father.*

JOHN 14:12 HCSB

In case you've been wondering whether or not you can do big things for God, you can stop wondering now. The Bible promises that you and the Lord, working together, can do amazing things.

How strong is God? He's much stronger than any of us can imagine. But even if we can't understand God's power, we can call on Him to give us the courage we need to follow His will.

The Lord has a wonderful plan for your life. And you can be sure that He will give you everything you need to accomplish all the things He plans for you to do.

☞ Remember This

You and God, working together, can accomplish great things for His kingdom. So pray as if everything depended on Him and work as if everything depended on you.

*** *** ***

226
God Looks on the Inside

God judges persons differently than humans do.
Men and women look at the face; GOD looks into the heart.

1 SAMUEL 16:7 MSG

We human beings are tempted to judge other people by the way they look on the outside. We pay attention to things like clothes and hair styles. But God makes His judgments differently. He looks on the inside— He examines the heart.

God doesn't care very much about the way you look or the clothes you wear, but He's very concerned about your soul. The Lord wants you to welcome Jesus into your heart, and He wants you to follow in Christ's footsteps.

So, the next time you find yourself worrying too much about your appearance, remember this: God is concerned, first and always, with what's on the inside, not what's on the outside.

☞ Remember This

God loves you and He wants you to follow the example of His Son. You should want the same thing, too.

✳ ✳ ✳
227
Trust Him

Trust the LORD with all your heart, and don't depend on your own understanding. Remember the Lord in all you do, and he will give you success.

PROVERBS 3:5–6 NCV

You can always trust God. Always. You can trust Him to handle the big things and the small things. You can turn all your cares and concerns over to Him And you can be sure that whenever He makes a promise, He will keep it.

God has big plans for you. And He has promised to protect you now and throughout eternity. So trust Him today, tomorrow, and always. When you do, you'll never be disappointed.

☞ Remember This

You can always trust God. He always keeps His promises. Always!

228
It's Time to Celebrate!

Celebrate God all day, every day.

PHILIPPIANS 4:4 MSG

What's the best day to celebrate God's gifts? This one! Today and every day should be a time for celebration as you think about all the wonderful things the Lord has done for you and your family.

Because you're a Christian, you have more blessings than you can possibly count, but it doesn't hurt to try. So today, as you take time to thank the Lord for His gifts, enjoy yourself. This day—like every other one—is a priceless gift from above. So celebrate!

 **A Timely Tip**

Every new day is a cause for celebration. It's up to you to join the celebration.

* * *
229
Don't Be Envious of Other People

*Where jealousy and selfishness are,
there will be confusion and every kind of evil.*

JAMES 3:16 NCV

Since God has already given you so many gifts—
and since He's already made so many promises to you
that He intends to keep—why should you be jealous of
anybody? The answer, of course, is that you shouldn't be!

The Bible teaches us that's it's wrong to envy other
people. But sometimes we become jealous when we see
folks who seem to have all the things we want.

Jealousy is a terrible waste of time and energy. So,
be thankful for the things you have, and don't worry too
much about the things that other people have. In other
words, count your own blessings, not your neighbor's.

* * *

*When you worry about what you don't have,
you won't be able to enjoy what you do have.*

CHARLES SWINDOLL

***

230
Focus on the Right Things

Keep your eyes focused on what is right,
and look straight ahead to what is good.

In the book of Proverbs, King Solomon gave great advice for living wisely. Solomon said that we should keep our eyes "focused on what is right." In other words, we should say and do what's pleasing to God.

The next time you're tempted to say an unkind word or to say something that isn't true, remember Solomon's advice. If you know you're about to make a mistake, don't do it. Instead, try your best to obey God's rules. When you do, you'll be saving yourself from many headaches, and you'll be obeying the Word of God.

***

Nobody is good by accident.

C. H. SPURGEON

✳ ✳ ✳
231
Share Your Enthusiasm!

Do your work with enthusiasm. Work as if you were serving
the Lord, not as if you were serving only men and women.

EPHESIANS 6:7 NCV

God wants you to work hard. But that's not all. He also wants you to be enthusiastic about your work, your life, your faith, and your future.

This world already has enough sadness. What it needs is more joy, more hope, and more enthusiasm. You can share these things with your family and friends—and you should.

Since you never know who might need a pat on the back or an encouraging word, be kind to everybody you meet. When you do, you'll make your corner of the world a better place. And God will bless you for it.

☞ Remember This

As a Christian, you have many reasons to be excited about your life and your future here on earth and in heaven. Share the excitement!

God Can Give You Courage

For God has not given us a spirit of fear and timidity,
but of power, love, and self-discipline.

2 TIMOTHY 1:7 NLT

If you're worried about something, you should always talk things over with your parents. And you should also talk to God. When you pray about the things that are bothering you, the Lord has a way of calming you down and cheering you up.

Sometimes the things that worry you are real problems, but other times, you may be concerned about something that's not really a problem at all. Your parents can help you sort out the big problems from the little ones. And God can help you, too. So don't hold your worries inside. Talk about them and pray about them. Today.

✳ ✳ ✳

In my experience, God rarely makes our fear disappear.
Instead, He asks us to be strong and take courage.

BRUCE WILKINSON

***

233
You Should Try to Please God

Do you think I am trying to make people accept me? No, God is the One I am trying to please. Am I trying to please people? If I still wanted to please people, I would not be a servant of Christ.

GALATIANS 1:10 NCV

The Bible says that we should always try to please God, not other people. But sometimes we're tempted to do the opposite: we're tempted to worry more about pleasing other people and less about pleasing God. That's a big mistake.

Are your friends the kind of kids who encourage you to behave yourself? If so, you've chosen your friends wisely. But if your friends try to get you in trouble, perhaps it's time to think long and hard about whom you're trying to please, and why.

Whether you know it or not, you're probably going to behave like your friends behave. So pick out friends who encourage you to put God first. When you do, you'll behave better and you'll feel better…a whole lot better.

☞ Remember This

People come and go, but God's love lasts forever. So don't worry about pleasing people. Worry about pleasing God.

✳ ✳ ✳

234
God Is Always with You

Do not be afraid or discouraged.
*For the L*ORD *your God is with you wherever you go.*

JOSHUA 1:9 NLT

God is everyplace. He's everywhere you've ever been, and He's everywhere you'll ever be. That's why you can talk to the Lord anytime you need to. And when you pray, you can be sure that He will hear you.

God promises to be by your side, now and forever. That's a promise you can trust. In fact, He's with you this very moment, waiting patiently to hear what you have to say. So why not have a word with Him right now?

✳ ✳ ✳

The best of all is, God is with us.

JOHN WESLEY

235
The Lord Wants You to Share

Oh, the joys of those who are kind to the poor!
The LORD rescues them when they are in trouble.

PSALM 41:1 NLT

The Lord has been very generous to you. Now, He wants you to give generously to people who need your help.

When you share, you're obeying God, and you're making your corner of the world a better place. Plus, you have the fun of knowing that your good deeds are making other people happy.

So when is the best time to share? Whenever you can—and that means right now, if possible. So don't delay; be generous today.

✳ ✳ ✳

We are never more like God than when we give.

CHARLES SWINDOLL

***

236
When You're Disappointed

Praise be to the God and Father of our Lord Jesus Christ. God is the Father who is full of mercy and all comfort. He comforts us every time we have trouble, so when others have trouble, we can comfort them with the same comfort God gives us.

2 CORINTHIANS 1:3–4 NCV

Some days are just plan wonderful. Everything seems to turn out right, and it's easy to praise God for all the good things that have happened. But other days aren't quite so happy. Sometimes bad things happen, and it makes you sad. But here's something to remember: even when you're disappointed with the way things have turned out, God is near, He's still in control, and He loves you very much!

If you're disappointed, sad, worried, or afraid, you can always talk things over with your parents, and you can talk to God. You'll certainly feel better when you do.

 **A Timely Tip**

When you're disappointed, ask God to help you find something new to become excited about. If you're looking forward to something in the future, you won't waste time worrying about past disappointments.

✳ ✳ ✳

237
Use Gentle Words

Always be humble, gentle, and patient,
accepting each other in love.

EPHESIANS 4:2 NCV

The Bible teaches us that angry words are harmful and gentle words are helpful. Of course, some people seem to make a habit of saying mean things, but as Christians, we are instructed to be thoughtful and kind.

So the next time you're tempted to say an unkind word, don't do it. And if you want to be a good example to your friends and family, remember that gentle words are better than harsh words and good deeds are better than the other kind.

✳ ✳ ✳

I choose gentleness. Nothing is won by force.
I choose to be gentle. If I raise my voice may it be only in praise.
If I clench my fist, may it be only in prayer.

MAX LUCADO

*** ☀ ☀

238
Since God Is Your Guide, You Can Be Confident

We can say with confidence,
"The LORD is my helper, so I will have no fear.
What can mere have no fear do to me?"

HEBREWS 13:6 NLT

God has promised to guide you and protect you. And since you can always trust God's promises, you should feel good—very good—about your future and your faith.

There's no limit to God's love, and there's no limit to the things He can do. So don't let occasional disappointments shake your confidence. As a Christian, you have many reasons to be optimistic and zero reasons to lose hope. You and God, working together, can do great things. You can be confident of that.

☞ Remember This

Confidence in yourself is fine, but what you need most of all is confidence in God.

239

Be Strong and Courageous

Be strong and courageous, and do the work.
Don't be afraid or discouraged, for the LORD God, my God,
is with you. He won't leave you or forsake you.

1 CHRONICLES 28:20 HCSB

Sometimes it takes courage to stand up for what you believe in. So, if you want to be a faithful Christian, you need to be strong.

You have lots of choices to make. Every day you must decide whether to honor God and obey His rules, or not. Whenever you're faced with a big decision—at home, at church, at school, or anyplace in between—be strong, be courageous, and take a stand for God. It's the right thing to do, and it's the best way to live.

✳ ✳ ✳

When God speaks, oftentimes His voice will
call for an act of courage on our part.

CHARLES STANLEY

240
How to Make Good Decisions

Anyone who listens to my teaching and follows it is wise,
like a person who builds a house on solid rock.

MATTHEW 7:24 NLT

Decisions, decisions, decisions. You make lots of them every day. When you make good decisions, you get good results. But if you make bad choices, you can be sure that trouble is right around the corner.

How can you learn to make good decisions? You can learn from your parents, of course. And you can learn from your teachers, too. But you should also learn from God.

The Bible is filled with stories about people who made choices. Sometimes people made good choices, and God rewarded them. But other Bible stories don't have such happy endings. So remember this: God still rewards good decisions and punishes poor ones. So choose carefully.

☞ Remember This

Want to make smart decisions? Then slow down and think about the consequences of your choices before you act, not after.

* * *
241
A Healthy Fear

Fear of the LORD is the foundation of true wisdom.
All who obey his commandments will grow in wisdom.

PSALM 111:10 NLT

The Bible teaches us that the fear of the Lord is the beginning of wisdom. When we have a healthy respect for God's power—and when we honor Him by obeying His commandments—we receive His approval and His blessings. But if we make the mistake of disobeying His commandments, we create problems for ourselves and for the people we love.

Do you have a healthy respect for your Father in heaven? If so, you're on the right track because until you have a respectful fear of God's power, your education is incomplete, and so is your faith.

* * *

A healthy fear of God will do much to deter us from sin.

CHARLES SWINDOLL

‫✳ ✳ ✳‬

242
Your Best Protection

Finally, be strong in the Lord and in his mighty power.
Put on the full armor of God, so that you can take
your stand against the devil's schemes.

EPHESIANS 6:10–11 NIV

There are so many ways that people can get into trouble. So how can you stay out of trouble? By putting God first and obeying His instructions, that's how.

The Bible says that when you "put on the full armor of God" you will be protected from things that get other people in trouble. God's armor isn't made out of metal or steel; it's the spiritual protection that He offers to those who love Him. When you put on God's armor, you'll be safe. So love the Lord with all your heart, say your prayers, and wear His armor every day of your life. It's the safe way to live.

✳ ✳ ✳

Under heaven's lock and key, we are protected by the most
efficient security system available: the power of God.

CHARLES SWINDOLL

243
You've Got Talent!

I remind you to fan into flames
the spiritual gift God gave you.

2 TIMOTHY 1:6 NLT

There's no doubt about it: You've got talent! Of course, you may not have figured out exactly which things you do best, but there will be plenty of time for that in the years to come. In the meantime, while you're trying to figure out exactly what you're good at, be sure and talk things over with your parents. They can help you decide how best to use and improve the gifts God has given you. And one more thing: be sure to thank your Father in heaven for the talents and blessings that make you a very special person to your family, to your friends, and to Him.

✳ ✳ ✳

In the great orchestra we call life,
you have an instrument and a song,
and you owe it to God to play them both sublimely.

MAX LUCADO

✳ ✳ ✳

244
It's Good to Cooperate

Work at getting along with each other and with God.
Otherwise you'll never get so much as a glimpse of God.

HEBREWS 12:14 MSG

It pays to be cooperative. When you help others, you feel better about yourself. And, since you know that God wants you to have a servant's heart, you can be sure that you've made the right choice.

When you learn how to cooperate with your family and friends, you'll soon discover that it's more fun when everybody works together. And one way that you can all work together is by sharing.

So do yourself a favor: learn better ways to share and better ways to cooperate. It's the right way to behave, and it's more fun, too.

✳ ✳ ✳

Teamwork makes the dream work.

JOHN MAXWELL

245
Learn to Think before You Speak

The wise don't tell everything they know,
but the foolish talk too much and are ruined.

PROVERBS 10:14 NCV

Ⅰt's easy to say the wrong thing if we're in a hurry to blurt out the first words that come into our heads. But if we're patient—and if we choose our words carefully— we can help other people feel better.

In Proverbs we are taught that the right words, spoken at the right time, can be wonderful gifts to our families and to our friends. That's why we should think about the things that we say before we say them, not after.

When you learn to think before you speak, you'll make your corner of the world a better place. And that's exactly what God wants you to do.

 **A Timely Tip**

If you can't think of something nice to say, keep thinking.

***
246
You Can't Please Everybody

Do you think I am trying to make people accept me?
No, God is the One I am trying to please.
Am I trying to please people? If I still wanted to please people,
I would not be a servant of Christ.

GALATIANS 1:10 NCV

*A*re you one of those boys who tries to please every-body in sight? If so, you'd better watch out! If you spend too much time trying to please your friends, you may not spend enough time pleasing God.

Your most important job is to obey God's rules (and that means obeying your parents, too). So don't worry too much about pleasing your friends or neighbors. Try, instead, to please your heavenly Father and your parents. You'll be glad you did...and so will they.

***

When our heart's desire is to please our Lord
because we love Him, there will be no time
for second thoughts or second opinions.

WARREN WIERSBE

* * *

247
Avoid Anger

*When you are angry, do not sin, and be sure to stop
being angry before the end of the day.
Do not give the devil a way to defeat you.*

EPHESIANS 4:26–27 NCV

The Bible tells us that we should control our tempers. And God's Word reminds us that temper tantrums always do more harm than good. But sometimes, especially when we're tired or frustrated, we may say things or do things that are unkind or hurtful to others. It's a big mistake, but it happens.

The next time you're tempted to strike out in anger, don't do it. Remember that gentle words are better than harsh words and good deeds are always better than the other kind.

* * *

Anger is the noise of the soul.

MAX LUCADO

248
It Pays to Worship God

But an hour is coming, and is now here, when the true worshipers will worship the Father in spirit and truth. Yes, the Father wants such people to worship Him. God is spirit, and those who worship Him must worship in spirit and truth.

JOHN 4:23–24 HCSB

It's good to worship God on Sunday mornings, but you shouldn't stop there. You should keep worshipping Him all throughout the week. How can you do it? You can worship Him all week long with your prayers, with your thoughts, and with your actions. So if you think that worship is something that only happens on Sundays, think again. You can worship God anywhere or anytime you feel the need to praise Him. And you should feel the need to praise Him every day.

✳︎ ✳︎ ✳︎

Worship is giving God the best that He has given you. Whenever you get a blessing from God, give it back to Him as a love gift.

OSWALD CHAMBERS

* * *

249
Beware of Pride

Pride leads only to shame; it is wise to be humble.

PROVERBS 11:2 NCV

When something good happens to you, it's tempting to take all the credit. It's tempting to say, "Look how great I am!" It's tempting, but it's wrong.

The Bible teaches us that too much pride can be a dangerous thing. When we try to take all the credit for the good things that happen to us, we forget to thank God. And He's the One who really deserves the praise, not us.

So the next time something good happens, don't praise yourself; praise your Father in heaven. It's the right thing to do.

☞ Remember This

A boy who's wrapped up in himself makes a very small package.

*** * ***

250
Make Good Choices
and Stay Out of Trouble

Praise the LORD! Happy are those who respect the LORD,
who want what he commands.

PSALM 112:1 NCV

God wants you to help other people, and He wants you to behave yourself, even when no grown-ups are around. But sometimes it's hard to do. Why? Because you may find yourself in a group of kids who are misbehaving. If it happens, you should remind yourself that God is watching and that your job is to please Him, not your friends.

Face facts: Not everybody you know is well-behaved. Your first job is to recognize bad behavior when you see it, and your second job is to make sure that you don't join in.

When you learn to avoid mischief, you'll please your Father in heaven, and you'll be glad you did!

*** * ***

Every day, I find countless opportunities to decide whether
I will obey God and demonstrate my love for Him or try to
please myself or the world system. God is waiting for my choices.

BILL BRIGHT

* * *
251
Your Attitude Makes a Big Difference

You must have the same attitude that Christ Jesus had.

PHILIPPIANS 2:5 NLT

God knows everything about you, including your attitude. When your attitude is good, God is pleased, and so are your family and friends.

Are you interested in pleasing God? Are you interested in pleasing your parents? Your teachers? Your friends? If so, try to make your attitude the best it can be. When you try hard to have a good attitude, you'll make other people feel better, and you'll make yourself feel better, too.

☞ Remember This

As a Christian, you have every reason on earth—and in heaven—to have a positive attitude.

* * *

252
Obeying God

Abundant peace belongs to those who love Your instruction;
nothing makes them stumble.

PSALM 119:165 HCSB

God has rules, and He wants you to obey them. The Lord wants you to be kind, fair, and honest. He wants you to behave like a Christian, and He wants you to respect your parents. God has other rules, too, and you'll find them in the book He wrote: the Holy Bible.

With a little help from your parents, you can figure out God's rules. Then, it's up to you to live by them. When you do, everybody will be pleased—you'll be pleased, your parents will be pleased, and God will be pleased, too.

* * *

Happiness is obedience, and obedience is happiness.

C. H. SPURGEON

✳ ✳ ✳

253
When You Are Hurting

But I will call on God, and the LORD will rescue me.
Morning, noon, and night I cry out in my distress,
and the LORD hears my voice.

PSALM 55:16–17 NLT

Most of the time, kids are pretty nice to each other, but sometimes they can be cruel. Some kids make fun of other children, and when they do, it's wrong. Period.

As Christians, we should be kind to everyone. And, if other kids say unkind things to a child or make fun of him or her, it's up to us to step in, like the Good Samaritan, and lend a helping hand.

If someone has hurt your feelings, you don't have to suffer in silence. You can talk things over with your parents, with your friends, and with God. And that's exactly what you should do. When you talk to a loved one about your troubles, you'll feel better. So don't hold in the hurt—talk about it!

 **A Timely Tip**

When you're hurting, when you're worried, or when you're afraid, talk to your parents. And while you're at it, talk to God about it, too.

254
Don't Give Up!

Though a righteous man falls seven times, he will get up,
but the wicked will stumble into ruin.

PROVERBS 24:16 HCSB

When you make a mistake, do you give up or do you keep trying? If you said, "I keep trying," you got the right answer.

Everybody makes mistakes, and you will, too. But when you allow a single mistake to slow you down—or cause you to stop altogether—you're making another, even bigger mistake.

Jesus didn't give up. He finished what He started, and so should you. So, the next time you're tempted to give up at the first sign of trouble, resist that temptation. When you keep trying, you'll discover that finishing is better than starting and determination does pay off.

 **A Timely Tip**

When you're tempted to give up, keep trying. If you quit at the first sign of trouble, you'll never know how good you can be.

255
Keep Trying

But endurance must do its complete work,
so that you may be mature and complete, lacking nothing.

JAMES 1:4 HCSB

*A*re you one of those boys who keeps going, even when it's hard? Or do you give up at the first sign of trouble? If you've developed the unfortunate habit of giving up too soon, it's probably time for you to have a heart-to-heart talk with the guy you see every time you look in the mirror.

The best things in life don't usually fall into our laps—we have to work for them. And if we don't succeed on the first try, we have to keep trying.

So the next time you're tempted to give up or give in, ask God to give you strength. Then try again, and keep trying until you get it right.

☝ Remember This

God never gives up on you, so don't you ever give up on Him.

✳ ✳ ✳

256

Be Respectful

*Show respect for all people: Love the brothers
and sisters of God's family.*

1 PETER 2:17 NCV

The Bible teaches us to be respectful, kind, and courteous. Should you show respect to grown-ups? Of course. Teachers? Certainly. Family members? Yes. Friends? Yes again. But it doesn't stop there. God wants us to treat all people with respect.

Respect for others is habitforming: the more you do it, the easier it becomes. So start practicing right now. Say kind words, do good deeds, and treat everybody you meet with the respect they deserve. You'll be glad you did, and God will be glad, too, because when it comes to kindness and respect, practice makes perfect.

✂ **Remember This**

God wants you to be respectful and courteous. When you respect other people, you're demonstrating your respect for God.

✳ ✳ ✳

257
Be a Trustworthy Friend

So stop telling lies. Let us tell our neighbors the truth,
for we are all parts of the same body.

EPHESIANS 4:25 NLT

Real friendships are built on both honesty and trust. Without trust, friends soon drift apart. But with trust, friends can stay friends for a lifetime.

When we treat other people with honesty and respect, we not only make more friends, but we also keep the friendships we've already made.

Do you want friends you can trust? Then start by being a friend they can trust. That's the way to make your friendships strong, stronger, and strongest!

 A Timely Tip

Lasting friendships are built on trust. If you want friends you can really trust, you must be a friend they can really trust.

✳✳✳
258
A Royal Law: Love Your Neighbor

Yes indeed, it is good when you obey
the royal law as found in the Scriptures:
"Love your neighbor as yourself."

JAMES 2:8 NLT

The Bible says that you should love your neighbor. In James, it says that when you love neighbor, you're obeying a "royal law." If you think that sounds important, you're right!

Can you honestly say that you're obeying God's royal law by loving your neighbors and treating them just like you'd want to be treated if you were in their shoes? If the answer is yes, you're on the right track. But if your answer is "maybe" or "sometimes," please slow down and pay careful attention to a very important law: the royal one.

✳✳✳

Encouraging others means helping people, looking for the
best in them, and trying to bring out their positive qualities.

JOHN MAXWELL

259
When Things Go Wrong

But as for you, be strong; don't be discouraged,
for your work has a reward.

2 CHRONICLES 15:7 HCSB

When things go wrong, do you give up at the first sign of trouble or do you keep trying? If you give up too quickly, you'll never know if you could have solved the problem. But if you keep trying, you might find out that your trouble was temporary—and you might succeed after all.

When you're disappointed or sad, it's easy to give up. But if you keep working and keep trying, you may be surprised at the things that you and God, working together, can do. So when in doubt, keep trying and keep praying. Who knows? Good things may be just around the corner.

✳ ✳ ✳

Prayer-time must be kept up as duly as meal-time.

MATTHEW HENRY

260
Honesty Pays

He who walks with integrity walks securely,
But he who perverts his ways will become known.

PROVERBS 10:9 NKJV

*A*n important part of growing up is learning how important it is to tell the truth. Lies usually have a way of hurting people, so even when it's hard, God wants you to be an honest person.

Honesty is not a "sometimes" thing. If you really want to please the Lord, you must form the habit of telling the truth all the time, not just some of the time.

Honesty pays and dishonesty doesn't. So if you want to follow God's rules, you must remember that truth is not just the best way, it is also His way. And you must act accordingly.

 **A Timely Tip**

When you're honest, people will respect you and trust you. So, always tell the truth, even when it's hard.

261
What's a Continual Feast?

A cheerful heart has a continual feast.

PROVERBS 15:15 HCSB

What is a continual feast? It's a little bit like a nonstop birthday party: lots and lots of fun! The Bible tells us that a happy heart can make life like a continual feast, and that's something worth working for.

You'll become a happier person when you remember to count your blessings every day. And you'll be happier when you behave yourself. So do yourself a favor: think good thoughts and do good deeds. When you do, your life will be like a continual feast...and you'll have even more things to be grateful for.

✳ ✳ ✳

The practical effect of Christianity is happiness, therefore let it be spread abroad everywhere!

C. H. SPURGEON

✳ ✳ ✳

262
Obey The Rules

We can be sure that we know God if we obey his commands.

1 JOHN 2:3 NCV

The Lord has rules that He wants you to obey. When you follow His instructions, you'll be protected. But if you disobey God, you're asking for trouble.

Do you listen to your heart when it tells you to behave yourself? Hopefully you do. After all, you'll be happier and healthier when you do the right thing.

So don't forget to listen to your conscience, to your parents, and to God. When you listen carefully, you'll be an obedient Christian, and you'll make everybody happy, including yourself!

 A Timely Tip

When you obey the rules, you'll be blessed. But if you disobey your Father in heaven, you must face the consequences. So, it's always wise to obey the rules—God's rules.

263
Kindness Starts with You

*And be kind and compassionate to one another, forgiving
one another, just as God also forgave you in Christ.*

EPHESIANS 4:32 HCSB

If you're waiting for other people to be nice to you before you're nice to them, you've got it backwards. Kindness starts with you!

You can never control what other people will say or do, but you can control your own behavior. You can choose to say kind things and do good deeds. And that's exactly what God wants you to do.

The Bible tells us to be courteous, kind, and respectful. Kindness is God's way, and it should be our way, too.

✳ ✳ ✳

*When you launch an act of kindness out into
the crosswinds of life, it will blow kindness back to you.*

DENNIS SWANBERG

* * *

264
God Can Do Anything

Is anything impossible for the Lord?

GENESIS 18:14 HCSB

Sometimes even the happiest Christians can become discouraged, and you are no exception. So, the next time you feel sad or fearful, remember that God can do anything, and He can solve any problem, including yours.

Every day, including this one, is loaded with opportunities to grow, to serve, and to share. Your job is to trust God and work hard. Focus on possibilities, fix your heart upon the Creator, do your best, and let Him handle the rest.

* * *

*God will give us the strength and resources
we need to live through any situation.*

BILLY GRAHAM

God Still Works Miracles

You are the God who works wonders;
You revealed Your strength among the peoples.

PSALM 77:14 HCSB

Sometimes, when we read about the amazing things that happened back in Bible times, we tell ourselves, "That was then, but this is now." When we think like that, we're mistaken. God is still actively involved in His world, and He's still performing miracles.

Miracles—both great and small—happen around us all day every day, but usually we're too busy to notice. Some miracles, like a twinkling star or a beautiful sunset, we take for granted. Other miracles we chalk up to fate or to luck. We think, incorrectly, that God is "out there" and we are "right here." Nothing could be further from the truth.

Instead of doubting God, trust His power and expect His miracles. Then, wait patiently, because something miraculous is about to happen…maybe sooner than you think.

✳ ✳ ✳

God is able to do what we can't do.

BILLY GRAHAM

266
Think Good Thoughts

Set your minds on what is above,
not on what is on the earth.

COLOSSIANS 3:2 HCSB

God wants us to think good thoughts, and He wants us to focus on Him, not the world. When we remind ourselves that God loves us, it's easy to feel better about the future because we know that God always keeps His promises.

Do you want to be happy and wise? Then you need to guard your thoughts against things that are hurtful or wrong. And while you're at it, remember this: when you turn away from bad thoughts and turn instead toward God, you will be protected, and you will be blessed.

* * *

The secret of living a life of excellence is merely
a matter of thinking thoughts of excellence.

CHARLES SWINDOLL

***

267
When Not to Follow the Crowd

My son, if sinners entice you, don't be persuaded.

PROVERBS 1:10 HCSB

If you're like most boys, you have probably been tempted to "go along with the crowd," even when the crowd was misbehaving. But here's something to think about: just because your friends misbehave doesn't mean that you have to misbehave, too.

When people behave badly, they can spoil things in a hurry. And it's your responsibility to make sure that they don't spoil things *for you*. So, if your friends misbehave, don't copy them! Instead, do the right thing. You'll be glad you did, your parents will be glad, and God will be glad, too.

***

If you try to be everything to everybody,
you will end up being nothing to anybody.

VANCE HAVNER

268
God Always Keeps His Promises

Let's keep a firm grip on the promises that keep us going.
He always keeps his word.

HEBREWS 10:23 MSG

Do you always keep your promises? Hopefully so. Do your friends always keep their promises? Sometimes yes, sometimes no. Do grown-ups always keep their promises? They try, but nobody's perfect. Nobody, that is, except God. He *always* keeps His promises.

Would you like to read a book that's filled with promises you can depend on? Then pick up your Bible and start reading! Every word of the Bible is true, and every promise will be fulfilled.

Your Bible is unlike any other book. Treat it that way—and do your best to read it every day.

☞ Remember This

God's promises never fail. He's going to keep every promise. You can depend on Him.

✳ ✳ ✳

269
Don't Be Afraid to Ask God for the Things You Need

Keep asking, and it will be given to you. Keep searching, and you will find. Keep knocking, and the door will be opened to you. For everyone who asks receives, and the one who searches finds, and to the one who knocks, the door will be opened.

MATTHEW 7:7–8 HCSB

What should you do if you really need something? Well, of course you can ask your parents, but you shouldn't stop there. You can also ask for God's help. When you do, you can be sure that He will hear your prayers.

The Bible makes it clear that when you need help, you can always turn to the Lord. You should ask for His help, but that's not all. You should also do your fair share of the work, trusting that when you've done your best, God will do the rest.

✳ ✳ ✳

Don't be afraid to ask your heavenly Father for anything you need. Indeed, nothing is too small for God's attention or too great for His power.

DENNIS SWANBERG

***

270
Jesus Offers Peace

Peace I leave with you. My peace I give to you.
I do not give to you as the world gives.
Your heart must not be troubled or fearful.

John 14:27 HCSB

The beautiful words of John 14:27 remind us that Jesus offers us peace, not as the world gives, but as He alone gives. We, as believers, can accept His peace or ignore it. When we accept the peace of Jesus Christ into our hearts, our lives are changed forever, and we become more loving, patient Christians.

Christ's peace is offered freely; it has already been-been paid for; it is ours for the asking. So let us ask…and then share.

***

The peace that Jesus gives is never engineered
by circumstances on the outside.

Oswald Chambers

271
Mountain-Moving Faith

For I assure you: If you have faith the size of a mustard seed,
you will tell this mountain, 'Move from here to there,'
and it will move. Nothing will be impossible for you.

MATTHEW 17:20 HCSB

Jesus told His disciples that if they had faith, they could move mountains. You can too. When you depend on God for your strength, anything is possible. If you trust the Lord and have faith in Him, you'll be amazed at the marvelous things He can do.

Are you a mountain-moving guy whose faith is evident for all to see? Hopefully so because God needs more people who are willing to move mountains for His glory and for His kingdom.

☞ Remember This

If your faith is strong enough, you and God—working together—can move mountains. No challenge is too big for God.

✳ ✳ ✳

272
How Do They Know?

Even children are known by their behavior;
their actions show if they are innocent and good.

PROVERBS 20:11 NCV

How do people know you're a Christian? Well, you can tell them, of course. That's one way they can learn about your faith, but it's not the only way or the best way. The best way to let people know that you're a Christian is to show them.

God doesn't just want you to become a Christian; He also wants you to behave like one. So please remember this: other people will learn about your faith from the words you say and the things you do, but not necessarily in that order.

In our faith we follow in someone's steps. In our faith we leave
footprints to guide others. It's the principle of discipleship.

MAX LUCADO

✳ ✳ ✳
273
A Thankful Heart

Enter his gates with thanksgiving; go into his courts
with praise. Give thanks to him and bless his name.
For the LORD is good. His unfailing love continues forever,
and his faithfulness continues to each generation.

PSALM 100:4–5 NLT

If you began counting your blessings, how long would it take? It would take a very long time. Your blessings include your life, your family, your talents, your possessions, and your friends. But, your greatest blessing—a gift that is yours for the asking—is God's gift of eternal life through His Son Jesus.

You can never count up every single blessing that the Lord has given you, but it doesn't hurt to try. So start counting your blessings right now...and keep counting them every day of your life.

 A Timely Tip

If you have a few spare minutes, don't reach for a smart phone or a TV clicker. Instead, reach out to God and say "thank You!"

✳ ✳ ✳

274
The Optimistic Christian

Make me hear joy and gladness.

PSALM 51:8 NKJV

What is an optimist? It's a person who looks for the best in others and believes that good things will probably happen soon. If you're a thinking Christian, you should be an optimistic Christian. After all, the Lord has promised to protect everybody who gives their hearts to Jesus. If that includes you, you have absolutely nothing to fear.

So be optimistic about your life, your faith, and your future. And while you're at it, share your optimism with others. They'll be better for it, and so will you. But not necessarily in that order.

Christ can put a spring in your step and a thrill in your heart. Optimism and cheerfulness are products of knowing Christ.

BILLY GRAHAM

* * *

275
Finding Time for God

I am always praising you; all day long I honor you.

PSALM 71:8 NCV

You're probably a very busy kid. You have things to do, things to see, and lots of things to learn. But here's a question: are you able to squeeze time into your schedule for God? Hopefully so!

Nothing is more important than the time you spend with the Lord. He will teach you and guide you if you let Him. So take some time today and every day to pray and to thank God for His blessings. Your heavenly Father will be glad you did, and you'll be glad, too.

* * *

Devotional books have an important ministry,
but they are never substitutes for your Bible.

WARREN WIERSBE

✳ ✳ ✳

276
God Is Faithful

I have set the LORD always before me;
because He is at my right hand I shall not be moved.

PSALM 16:8 NKJV

God is always faithful. He keeps His promises; He never stops loving us; and He never leaves us, not even for a moment.

Wherever you go today, God will be there, too, always watching over you, always trying to lead you along the proper path: His path. So please remember that the Lord is always faithful to you, and you, in turn, must be faithful to Him.

✳ ✳ ✳

I have a great need for Christ;
I have a great Christ for my need.

C. H. SPURGEON

✳ ✳ ✳

277
Obey God's Rules

For this is what love for God is: to keep His commands.
Now His commands are not a burden, because whatever
has been born of God conquers the world.
This is the victory that has conquered the world: our faith.

1 JOHN 5:3–4 HCSB

God has rules, and He wants you to obey them. He wants you to be friendly, kind, and honest. He wants you to behave yourself, and He wants you to respect your parents. God has other rules, too, and you'll find them in a very special book: the Holy Bible.

With a little help from your parents, you can figure out God's rules. And then, with a little help from above, you can live by His rules. When you do, everybody will be pleased—you'll be pleased, your parents will be pleased, and the Lord will be pleased, too.

✳ ✳ ✳

To be a Christian means to forgive the inexcusable,
because God has forgiven the inexcusable in you.

C. S. LEWIS

✳ ✳ ✳

278
God Is Love

The one who does not love does not know God,
because God is love.

1 JOHN 4:8 HCSB

The Bible teaches us that God is love. And how much does God love you? He loves you so much that He sent His Son Jesus to come to this earth for you! And, when you accept Jesus into your heart, God gives you a gift that is more precious than gold: that gift is called "eternal life," which means that you will live forever with God in heaven.

God's love is bigger and more powerful than anybody can imagine, but it is very real. So do yourself a favor right now: accept God's love with open arms and welcome His Son Jesus into your heart. When you do, your life will be changed today, tomorrow, and forever.

☞ Remember This

God's love never fails. You can always depend upon Him because He always keeps His promises. Always.

‗ ✳ ✳ ✳

279
Follow Jesus

*"Follow Me," Jesus told them, "and I will make you
fish for people!" Immediately they
left their nets and followed Him.*

MARK 1:17–18 HCSB

Jesus wants to have a real relationship with you. Are you willing to have a real relationship with Him? Unless you can answer this question with a resounding "yes," you may miss out on some wonderful things.

This day offers yet another opportunity to behave yourself like a real Christian. When you do, God will guide your steps and bless your endeavors forever. So don't delay; follow Jesus today!

✳ ✳ ✳

*Discipleship is a daily discipline:
we follow Jesus a step at a time, a day at a time.*

WARREN WIERSBE

Getting to Know Jesus

Then Jesus said, "I am the bread that gives life.
Whoever comes to me will never be hungry,
and whoever believes in me will never be thirsty."

JOHN 6:35 NCV

There's really no way around it: If you want to know God, you need to know His Son. And that's good, because getting to know Jesus can—and should—be a wonderful experience.

Jesus has amazing love for you. Have you thought about exactly what His love means? It means that you can live forever with Him in heaven. That's why Christ's love should make you feel better about your life, your family, your future, and yourself. So, welcome Jesus into your heart today. When you do, you'll always be grateful that you did.

✳ ✳ ✳

When you can't see Him, trust Him.
Jesus is closer than you ever dreamed.

MAX LUCADO

281
The Power of Prayer

Therefore I say to you, whatever things you ask when you pray, believe that you receive them, and you will have them.

MARK 11:24 NKJV

Your prayers are powerful! When you pray hard and have faith in God, great things can happen. Of course, God doesn't always answer your prayers right away, and He doesn't always give you everything you want, exactly when you want it. But He does promise to hear your prayers, and He promises to guide you along the right path: His path.

So, the next time you bow your head to pray, remember that you're talking to the Creator of the universe...and remember that when you talk to the Lord, you're having a *very* important conversation.

✳ ✳ ✳

Prayer is the hard-work business of Christianity, and it nets amazing results.

DAVID JEREMIAH

✳ ✳ ✳

282
When in Doubt, Ask and Pray

Don't depend on your own wisdom.
Respect the LORD and refuse to do wrong.

PROVERBS 3:7 NCV

If you're not sure what to do, who can you ask? You should talk to your parents, of course. And if you're in school, you can talk to your teachers. But you can also pray about your questions, and sometimes God will give you His answer loud and clear.

The Lord has given you a conscience—a little voice inside your head—that tells you right from wrong. So if you have a question, you should listen to your conscience, too.

When you have questions there are trusted places you can go for the answers you need. So don't be afraid to ask.

☞ Remember This

If you're not sure what to do, pray about it. And talk to your parents as soon as you can. God wants to hear from you, and so do your parents.

* * *

283
When People Misbehave

*You have heard that it was said, Love your neighbor
and hate your enemy. But I tell you, love your enemies
and pray for those who persecute you,
so that you may be sons of your Father in heaven.*

MATTHEW 5:43–45 HCSB

Sometimes people can be cruel. And sometimes they can be rude. And sometimes they misbehave. Why? Because none of us are perfect. As long as you live here on earth, you will face countless opportunities to lose your temper when other folks behave badly. But God has a better plan: He wants you to forgive everybody and move on.

Remember that God has already forgiven you, so it's only right that you should be willing to forgive other people when they hurt you.

* * *

*There is no use in talking as if forgiveness were easy.
I could say of a certain man, "Have I forgiven him more
times than I can count?" For we find that the work
of forgiveness has to be done over and over again.*

C. S. LEWIS

✳ ✳ ✳

284
Honesty Starts at Home

The godly are directed by honesty.

PROVERBS 11:5 NLT

Should you be honest with your parents? Of course. With your brothers and sisters? Certainly. With cousins, grandparents, aunts, and uncles? Once again, the answer is yes. In fact, you should be honest with everybody in your family because honesty starts at home.

If you can't be honest in your own house, how can you expect to be honest in other places, like at church or at school? So make sure that you're always honest with your family. If you are, then you're much more likely to be honest with everybody else.

☞ Remember This

Sometimes telling the truth is hard. But it's not nearly as hard as telling a lie and living with a guilty conscience.

285
Praising God's Glorious Universe

The heavens declare the glory of God,
and the sky proclaims the work of His hands.

PSALM 19:1 HCSB

When you look at the night sky, do you ever think about how amazing God is? After all, He created all the stars you can see plus zillions more that you can't see. He made everything in the whole universe: the stars, the planets, the sun, the moon, and you.

When the Lord created you, He gave you a mind that is able to understand the beauty of His handiwork. So the next time you look up at the starts, please remember that God made all that…and give Him the praise He deserves.

👉 Remember This

The more carefully you inspect God's unfolding universe, the more beautiful it becomes.

✳ ✳ ✳
286
The Best Time to Help

*Truly I tell you, whatever you did for one of the least
of these brothers and sisters of mine, you did for me.*

MATTHEW 25:40 NIV

Two thousand years ago, Christ told His followers that they should help people in need. And if we want to follow Christ today, we should do likewise. As Christians, our instructions are clear: we must help those who are less fortunate than we are.

Jesus said that whenever we help needy people, it's as if we were helping Him. And that's a good enough reason to be generous and kind. So today and every day, be generous and kind. And be quick to help people who cannot help themselves. It's the best way to give and the best way to live.

👉 Remember This

When people are unable to help themselves, you can—and should—help them. When you do, Jesus says it's exactly like helping Him.

✳ ✳ ✳
287
God Has a Plan for You

And don't be wishing you were someplace else or with someone else. Where you are right now is God's place for you. Live and obey and love and believe right there.

1 CORINTHIANS 7:17 MSG

Here are three things for you to think about:
1. God loves you.
2. God wants what's best for you.
3. God has a plan for you.

The Bible tells us God's plans are far bigger than we humans can possibly understand. But even when we can't understand why the Lord allows certain things to happen, we can trust His love for us. So even if you don't get exactly what you want today, you can be sure that God has something better in store for you tomorrow.

✳ ✳ ✳

It's incredible to realize that what we do each day has meaning in the big picture of God's plan.

BILL HYBELS

* * *

288
This Is the Day

*This is the day the L*ord *has made; let us rejoice and be glad in it.*

Psalm 118:24 HCSB

Today is God's gift to you. The Lord has given you another day of life, and He wants you to rejoice and be glad.

For Christians, every day begins and ends with God and with His Son. Christ came to this earth to give us hope, joy, peace, and eternal life. As we share Christ's Good News with our family and friends, we're reminded of how much He loves us.

So, what will you do today? Will you celebrate God's blessings and obey His commandments? Will you share kind words with the people who cross your path? Will you pray often and thank the Lord for more blessings than you can count? Only you can answer these questions. Please answer wisely.

* * *

Why wait until the fourth Thursday in November? Why wait until the morning of December twenty-fifth? Thanksgiving to God should be an everyday affair. The time to be thankful is now!

Jim Gallery

✳ ✳ ✳
289
The Power of Our Thoughts

People's thoughts can be like a deep well, but someone
with understanding can find the wisdom there.

PROVERBS 20:5 NCV

Your thoughts are powerful because they have so much control over the things you say and the things you do. No wonder God wants you to think good thoughts!

When you focus on things that bring you closer to the Lord, you'll feel better about yourself, and you'll feel better about your world. But if you watch things—or think about things—that are harmful, hurtful, or scary, you'll feel worse, not better.

Today and every day, guard your thoughts and be careful what you watch. When you do, you'll be a happier person and a better Christian.

Your thoughts are the determining factor as to whose
mold you are conformed to. Control your thoughts
and you control the direction of your life.

CHARLES STANLEY

＊ ＊ ＊

290
The Joys of a Clear Conscience

Let us come near to God with a sincere heart and a sure faith,
because we have been made free from a guilty conscience,
and our bodies have been washed with pure water.

HEBREWS 10:22 NCV

When you know you've done the right thing, you'll feel better about yourself. But if you've made a mistake—and if you're still trying to hide it—you won't feel very good. So here's a simple rule that can improve your day and your life: always trust your conscience, and when it says stop, don't go.

When you have a clear conscience, you'll be a happier person. So trust your conscience and listen to it. When you do, you'll always be glad.

To go against one's conscience is neither safe nor right.
Here I stand. I cannot do otherwise.

MARTIN LUTHER

* * *
291
Forgive One Another

Be gentle with one another, sensitive. Forgive one another as quickly and thoroughly as God in Christ forgave you.

EPHESIANS 4:32 MSG

When other people behave badly, it's hard to forgive them, but that's exactly what God tells us to do. How hard is it to forgive? Sometimes it's very hard, but God instructs us to forgive other people even when we'd rather not. So, if you're angry with anybody (or if you're upset by something you yourself have done), it's time to forgive. Right now!

God instructs you to treat other people exactly as you wish to be treated. And since you want to be forgiven for the mistakes that you make, you must be willing to extend forgiveness to other people for the mistakes that they have made. If you can't seem to forgive someone, you should keep asking God to help you until you do. And you can be sure of this: if you keep asking for God's help, He will give it.

👉 Remember This

The best time to forgive somebody is as soon as possible, if not sooner!

✳ ✳ ✳

292
When Things Go Wrong

Be joyful because you have hope. Be patient
when trouble comes, and pray at all times.

ROMANS 12:12 NCV

When things go wrong, do you give up at the first sign of trouble? Or do you moan, groan, whine, and complain? If so, please remember that complaining doesn't fix anything.

The Bible promises that God can take your troubles and turn them into victories. That means there's a good chance that God may be using your problems today in order to help you become a better person tomorrow.

So don't cry about your troubles and don't complain about them. Instead, do your best to fix them. And when you've done all that you can, leave the rest up to God.

✳ ✳ ✳

Each problem is a God-appointed instructor.

CHARLES SWINDOLL

293

When You Don't Know What to Say

To everything there is a season...
a time to keep silence, and a time to speak.

ECCLESIASTES 3:1,7 KJV

Sometimes it's hard to know exactly what to say. And sometimes it can be very tempting to say something that isn't true, or something that isn't nice. But if you say things you shouldn't say, you'll regret it later.

So make this promise to yourself, and keep it— promise to think about the things you say before you say them. And if you can't think of something nice to say, don't say anything at all. When you do these things, you'll be doing yourself and your friends a big favor. But more importantly, you'll be obeying the Word of God.

A Timely Tip

When you're not sure what to say, it's perfectly okay to keep your mouth tightly closed. It's better to say nothing than to say something you'll regret later.

✳ ✳ ✳
294
You're Always Growing Up

*Grow in the grace and knowledge of our Lord and Savior
Jesus Christ. All glory to him, both now and forever! Amen.*

2 PETER 3:18 NLT

God's plan for you includes a lifetime of prayer,
praise, worship, and growth. The Lord doesn't want you
to stand still in your faith. He wants you to keep growing,
and growing, and growing, both as a person and as a
Christian.

When will you be "fully grown"? Not until you get
to heaven. So don't worry if you still have lots to learn.
You still have plenty of time to learn the lessons that your
heavenly Father wants to teach you.

Remember This

Learning is fun! You can always learn something
new...and that's what God wants you to do.

295
Trust God to Teach You What's Right

Depend on the LORD in whatever you do,
and your plans will succeed.

PROVERBS 16:3 NCV

The Lord has many things He wants to teach you, but He won't force you to learn. God doesn't make you read your Bible; He doesn't insist that you listen to your parents or your teachers; and He doesn't force you to learn from your mistakes. Instead, God lets you decide whether to learn…or not.

You're never too young—or too old—to learn something new. And, the Lord still has lessons that He intends to teach you. So ask yourself this question: "What is God trying to teach me today?"

☞ Remember This

The Bible teaches you right from wrong. So when you're about to make an important choice, slow down and have a little chat with God. His way is always the right way.

✳✳✳
296
Don't Worship Stuff

No one can serve two masters. The person will hate one master and love the other, or will follow one master and refuse to follow the other. You cannot serve both God and worldly riches.

MATTHEW 6:24 NCV

One of the easiest idols to worship is the idol called money. Some people will do almost anything to get more money—don't you dare be one of them!

Money isn't important to God, and it shouldn't be very important to you. After all, God knows that His children will live with Him forever in heaven, so He's not too concerned about earthly possessions, which are here today and gone tomorrow. So the next time you find yourself worrying about the stuff you own or the things you want to buy, remember that you should worship God, not your possessions. Your *real* treasure is in heaven.

☞ Remember This

The things you own are temporary. God's love is permanent. Put God first, and don't spend much time worrying about your possessions.

Put Jesus in Your Heart Today and Every Day

I tell you the truth, anyone who believes has eternal life.

JOHN 6:47 NLT

God loves you. In fact, His love for you is so great that He sent His only Son to die for your sins and offer you the priceless gift of eternal life. Now, it's up to you to welcome Jesus into your heart and accept His incredible gift.

It's always the right time to accept God's gift and assure your place in heaven. So, if you haven't already done so, please make Jesus your Ssavior right now. Jesus loves you, and He wants you to return His love…right now.

✳ ✳ ✳

*Turn your life over to Christ today,
and your life will never be the same.*

BILLY GRAHAM

298
God Has Prepared
a Place for You in Heaven

Be glad and rejoice, because your reward is great in heaven.

MATTHEW 5:12 HCSB

The Bible promises that when you give your heart to Jesus, you will live forever with Him in heaven. So what will heaven be like? We can't be sure about the details, but we can be certain that heaven is a wonderful place, a place filled with joy, a place where we will be reunited with our loved ones. Heaven is a priceless gift from God. Let's be sure to thank Him every day for the gift of life.

☞ Remember This

Heaven is real, and the Lord has prepared a place for you there. When you welcome Jesus into your heart, God has promised that you'll spend eternity in heaven. What an amazing promise...and what an amazing place!

*** *** ***

299
It Helps to Be Helpful

Two people are better than one,
because they get more done by working together.

ECCLESIASTES 4:9 NCV

Over and over again, the Bible teaches us that we should help each other. God's Word makes it clear that we should be kind to each other, and that we should co-operate with our families and friends.

If you want to make your corner of the world a better place, remember that it helps to be helpful. Make yourself helpful at school, at church, and at home. When you do, you'll feel better about yourself, and other people will be grateful. So don't delay; be helpful today.

 A Timely Tip

When you help other people, you'll feel better about yourself. And you'll be blessed because you've obeyed God's instructions. So what are you waiting for?

300
Learn to Control Yourself

All athletes are disciplined in their training.
They do it to win a prize that will fade away,
but we do it for an eternal prize.

1 CORINTHIANS 9:25 NLT

Learning to control yourself is an important part of growing up. Self-control will help you at home, at school, at church, and just about everyplace else you can think of.

Maybe you're one of those people who tries to do everything fast, faster, or fastest! If that's the case, it's probably a good idea to slow down a little bit so you can think before you act. And while you're at it, it's probably a good idea to think before you speak, too. After all, you'll never have to apologize for something that you didn't say.

Remember This

If you learn to control yourself, you'll earn big rewards. If you can't learn to control yourself, you'll have lots of problems. Behave accordingly.

* * *

301
Sharing Your Stuff

Freely you have received, freely give.

MATTHEW 10:8 NKJV

Jesus taught us to be generous and to share the things we have. But sometimes we don't feel much like sharing. Instead of being cheerful givers, we want to keep everything for ourselves.

Do you have lots of nice things? If so, God's instructions are clear: you must share your blessings with others. And that's exactly the way it should be. After all, think how generous God has been with you.

* * *

Nothing is really ours until we share it.

C. S. LEWIS

302
Keep Doing Good Deeds

Carry one another's burdens;
in this way you will fulfill the law of Christ.

GALATIANS 6:2 HCSB

How many good deeds should you do in a day? Is one enough? Or two? Or ten? The answer can't be summed up in a single number. Why? Because God wants you to do as many good deeds as you can, and He knows that you have many opportunities each day to say a kind word or lend a helping hand.

Today and every day, try to do as many good deeds as you can. Keep your eyes open wide and look for people to serve. When you do, you'll make everybody happy, and you'll please your Father in heaven.

Remember This

When you're helping somebody else, you're actually serving God.

***

303
Two Bible Verses to Memorize

Today, try to memorize these verses from the Bible:

*Therefore, whatever you want others
to do for you, do also the same for them—
this is the Law and the Prophets.*

MATTHEW 7:12 HCSB

*I can do all things through Christ
who strengthens me.*

PHILIPPIANS 4:13 NKJV

If You Want to Be a Good Person, You Can Do It!

Those who hunger and thirst for righteousness are blessed, for they will be filled.

Matthew 5:6 HCSB

Sometimes it's hard to do the right thing...but it's not impossible. You can always choose to obey God, and you always should. Of course your world is filled with so many distractions—television shows, games, and other kinds of media—that you could spend a whole lifetime in front of a screen, paying almost no attention to God's rules or God's Son. But that would be a huge mistake.

Today, remember that when God asks you to be a good person, He's not asking you to do something that's impossible. He's asking you to do something that's smart. Then, behave accordingly.

☞ Remember This

It's always possible to do the right thing, and it's always possible to obey God. The Lord will teach you and guide you if you ask. So ask!

* * *

305
God Will Protect You

God's power protects you through your faith until salvation is shown to you at the end of time.

1 PETER 1:5 NCV

When bad things happen, it's easy to get discouraged. But if you're a Christian, there's no need to stay discouraged for long. Why? Because God has promised to protect you now and forever, and He's certainly going to keep that promise.

So the next time you're worried or afraid, remember this: God is always with you and He loves you. Whether your problem is a big one or a small one, He's big enough and strong enough to handle it. The Lord is your Shepherd, and He's promised to watch over you today, tomorrow, and throughout eternity. Trust the Shepherd.

☞ Remember This

God has promised to protect you, and He's going to keep that promise. So if you're worried or afraid, pray about it.

306
Prayerful Patience

The LORD is good to those who wait for Him,
to the person who seeks Him.

<small>LAMENTATIONS 3:25 HCSB</small>

If you'd like to become a more patient person, ask God to help you. Talk to Him in prayer, listen carefully for His answers, and follow as closely as you can in the footsteps of His Son.

God always hears your prayers and He's always ready to help you become a better person. In fact, Your heavenly Father is listening, and He's ready to talk to you now. So don't make Him wait. Talk to Him about the things you need and the person you want to become. When you ask—and keep asking—He will help you become that person.

☞ Remember This

If you'd like to become a more patient person, pray about it. God can help you do things that you can't do by yourself.

*** *** ***

307
It's Good to Forgive

All bitterness, anger and wrath, insult and slander must
be removed from you, along with all malice.
And be kind and compassionate to one another, forgiving
one another, just as God also forgave you in Christ.

EPHESIANS 4:31–32 HCSB

God wants you to forgive the people who have hurt you. And when you forgive somebody, you're actually doing yourself a favor. Why? Because when you forgive the other person, you get rid of angry feelings that can make you unhappy.

Are you still angry about something that happened yesterday, or the day before that, or the day before that? If so, please do yourself a big favor: forgive everybody (including yourself, if necessary). When you do, you won't change what happened yesterday, but you will make today a whole lot better.

☞ Remember This

Forgiveness is a gift you give to another person and to yourself, but not necessarily in that order.

308
Keep Asking

So I say to you, keep asking, and it will be given to you.
Keep searching, and you will find. Keep knocking,
and the door will be opened to you.

Luke 11:9 HCSB

How often should you ask God for the things you really need? Once? Twice? Ten times? The Bible teaches us that we should ask God—and keep asking Him—for the things we need. If that means asking Him a hundred times, that's okay. Even a thousand prayerful requests won't bother Him in the least.

God can do great things through you if you have the courage to ask Him (and the determination to keep asking Him). But don't expect Him to do all the work. When you do your part, He will do His part—and when He does, you can expect miracles to happen.

✳ ✳ ✳

Some people think God does not like
to be troubled with our constant asking.
But, the way to trouble God is not to come at all.

D. L. Moody

✳ ✳ ✳

309
Choose Your Friends Carefully

Walk with the wise and become wise;
associate with fools and get in trouble.

PROVERBS 13:20 NLT

The world is filled with pressures: some good, some bad. The pressures that we feel to follow God's rules are the good kind of pressures (and the friends who make us want to obey God are good friends). But sometimes we may feel pressure to misbehave, pressure from friends who want us to disobey the rules.

If you want to please God and your parents, make friends with people who behave themselves. When you do, you'll be much more likely to behave yourself, too... and that's a very good thing.

 **A Timely Tip**

If you choose friends wisely, you'll soon be blessed. If you choose friends unwisely, you'll soon be in a mess.

* * *

310

Pay Attention in School! (and Other Places, Too)

Remember what you are taught,
and listen carefully to words of knowledge.

PROVERBS 23:12 NCV

When you pay attention—at school, at church, at home, or just about anyplace else—you can learn a lot. The better you listen, the more you'll learn. But sometimes, as you've probably figured out by now, it's hard to pay attention. Why? Because your world is filled with lots of distractions.

So what, exactly, is a distraction? It's anything that grabs your attention when you should be paying attention to something else. Sometimes friends can distract you. Sometimes TV can distract you. Sometimes games can distract you. And sometimes you can even distract yourself.

If you think about distractions before they happen, you're better prepared to handle them. So be on the lookout for distractions. It's the smart way to learn and the best way to live.

Remember This

You can learn things at school, at home, at church, and lots of other places, too. So keep your eyes and ears open. When you do, you'll get smarter every day.

✳ ✳ ✳

311
Do Good Deeds Now

So let's not tired of doing what is good.
At just the right time we will reap
a harvest of blessing if we don't give up.

GALATIANS 6:9 NLT

When is the best time to do good deeds? The answer, of course, is as soon as you can!

God has important things for you to do, and He wants you to be an important part of His plan. But the Lord allows you to make choices every day, and He doesn't force you to obey His rules.

Today and every day, try to make your corner of the world a better place. When you do, you'll make other people happy, and you'll make God happy, too.

👉 Remember This

The Bible teaches us to be "doers of the Word, not merely hearers." The best time to obey God's Word—and the very best time to serve Him—is now.

❋ ❋ ❋

312
God Is Bigger Than Your Troubles

Be joyful because you have hope.
Be patient when trouble comes, and pray at all times.

ROMANS 12:12 NCV

If you have a problem—or if something scares you—talk to your parents! Your parents love you and care for you, and they will protect you. And it's the same with God. You can talk to Him about your troubles, too. When you pray, God will listen. And He's promised to protect you now and forever.

So if you have a problem, there's always somebody you can talk to. You can talk to your parents, and you can talk to God. Please don't keep things to yourself; start talking *now*.

 **A Timely Tip**

When considering the size of your problems, there are two categories that you should never worry about: the problems that are small enough for you to handle, and the ones that aren't too big for God to handle.

* * *

313
How Much Is Too Much?

*Since we entered the world penniless and will leave
it penniless, if we have bread on the table
and shoes on our feet, that's enough.*

1 TIMOTHY 6:7–8 MSG

How much stuff is too much stuff? Think of it like this: if your desire for stuff is getting in the way of your desire to know God, then you've got too much stuff—it's as simple as that.

The world keeps pumping out messages that say you need to buy things in order to be happy. But real happiness can't be purchased in a store; it can only come from the heart. So if you find yourself worrying too much about the things you own—or about the things you don't own but wish you did—it's time for an attitude adjustment. Stuff isn't really very important to God, and it shouldn't be too important to you.

* * *

*If you want to be truly happy, you won't find it on an endless
quest for more stuff. You'll find it in receiving God's generosity
and in the passing that generosity along.*

BILL HYBELS

314
Don't Whine

Do everything without complaining or arguing.
Then you will be innocent and without any wrong.

PHILIPPIANS 2:14–15 NCV

What's an attitude? The word "attitude" means "the way that you think." And don't forget this: your attitude is important.

Your attitude can make you happy or sad, grumpy or glad, joyful or mad. And, your attitude doesn't just control the way that you think; it also controls how you behave. If you have a good attitude, you'll behave well. But if you have a bad attitude, you're more likely to misbehave.

Some people are tempted to complain, and whine, and do very little else. Please don't act that way. Instead of whining about your problems, get busy solving them. When you do, you'll soon discover that good thoughts, accompanied by good deeds, lead to good results, but that whining usually leads elsewhere.

Remember This

You'll never whine your way to the top, so don't even try.

✳︎✳︎✳︎

315
You Can Trust God's Word

But He answered, "It is written: Man must not live on bread
alone, but on every word that comes from the mouth of God."

MATTHEW 4:4 HCSB

The words of Matthew 4:4 remind us that God's instructions are important. The Bible is an amazing roadmap designed to teach us about life here on earth—which is temporary—and life in heaven, which lasts forever. As a Christian, you are instructed to read God's holy Word, to follow its commandments, and to share its Good News with the people you meet.

The Bible is a priceless gift from our Lord. That's why good Christians (like you) must never live by bread alone, but also by every word that comes from God's one-of-a-kind holy guidebook.

✳︎✳︎✳︎

God has given us all sorts of counsel and direction
in his written Word; thank God, we have
it written down in black and white.

JOHN ELDREDGE

***

316
What Kind of Example?

You should be an example to the believers in speech,
in conduct, in love, in faith, in purity.

1 TIMOTHY 4:12 HCSB

What kind of example are you? Are you the kind of boy who shows other kids what it means to be kind and forgiving? Hopefully so.

How hard is it to say a kind word? Not very. How hard is it to accept someone's apology? Usually not too hard. So today, be a good example for others to follow.

God wants people like you to stand up and be counted for Him. And that's exactly the kind of example He wants you to be.

☞ Remember This

The words you choose and the choices you make will have big impact on your friends and family. Be sure that your words and your choices are pleasing to God and helpful to your loved ones.

* * *

317
The Right Kind of Friends

Spend time with the wise and you will become wise,
but the friends of fools will suffer.

PROVERBS 13:20 NCV

Do your friends encourage you to behave yourself? If so, you've chosen the right friends.

But if your friends are constantly getting you in trouble, perhaps it's time to think long and hard about making some new friends.

Whether you know it or not, you'll probably behave like your friends behave. So pick friends who encourage you to behave like a Christian. When you do, you'll avoid plenty of problems, and you'll become a better person because of the friends you've chosen.

* * *

A friend is one who makes me do my best.

OSWALD CHAMBERS

✳ ✳ ✳

318
Every Day Is a Special Day

*This is the day that the L*ORD *has made.*
Let us rejoice and be glad today!

PSALM 118:24 NCV

Today is a special day. Why? Because God made it and filled it with opportunities to serve Him and to follow in the footsteps of His Son.

This day—like every other day—is a time to rejoice and thank God for all the wonderful things He has done. So don't wait for birthdays or holidays—make every day a special day, including this one. And while you're at it, slow down long enough to praise your heavenly Father. It pays to praise, and it pays to celebrate...*now!*

 **A Timely Tip**

Today, like every other day, is a gift from God. Treat it that way.

319

Jesus Doesn't Want You to Worry

So don't worry about tomorrow, because tomorrow will have its own worries. Each day has enough trouble of its own.

MATTHEW 6:34 NCV

In the sixth chapter of Matthew, Jesus teaches us that we shouldn't worry about the small stuff, things like the food we eat or the clothes we wear. Instead, Christ asks us to focus on the important things, like God's promises and God's love.

It's easy to worry about things—big things, little things, and in-between things, too. But the Bible promises that if you learn to trust the Lord more and more each day, you have no need to worry. If God is powerful enough to create the universe and everything in it, He's also strong enough to take care of you. Now that's a comforting thought!

✳ ✳ ✳

The closer you live to God, the smaller your worries appear.

RICK WARREN

✳ ✳ ✳

320
Pray and Keep Praying

Rejoice always, pray without ceasing, in everything give thanks; for this is the will of God in Christ Jesus for you.

1 THESSALONIANS 5:16–18 NKJV

How often should you pray? Once a day? Twice? At bedtimes and mealtimes? The Bible says that you should pray much more than that.

The Bible teaches us that we should "pray without ceasing." That means we should say many prayers throughout the day. If that sounds like a lot of work, don't worry. It really isn't that hard.

God hears all your prayers, not just the ones you pray when your eyes are closed. You can talk to the Lord anytime you want, and you can keep your eyes open if you need to.

So don't be satisfied to pray once or twice a day. Keep praying all day long. You'll be glad you did.

✳ ✳ ✳

Prayer succeeds when all else fails.

E. M. BOUNDS

And the Greatest of These...

So these three things continue forever:
faith, hope, and love. And the greatest of these is love.

1 CORINTHIANS 13:13 NCV

First Corinthians 13 is an important chapter in the Bible because it reminds us that God wants us to be loving and kind. Faith is important to God. And hope is important, too. But love is greatest gift of all.

Jesus showed His love on the cross, and now it's up to us to return His love by sharing it. So do yourself—and everybody else—a favor: share Christ's love today.

✳ ✳ ✳

Because God is love, the most important lesson
He wants you to learn on earth is how to love.

RICK WARREN

322

Trust Your Conscience and Do the Right Thing

Don't let evil get the best of you;
get the best of evil by doing good.

ROMANS 12:21 MSG

What is your conscience? Some people describe it as a little voice, but you can also think of it as a feeling— a feeling that tells you whether something is right or wrong. Your conscience will tell you what to do and when to do it. Your job is to listen and to learn.

If you listen to your conscience, you'll usually stay out of trouble, so don't be in such a hurry to do things. Instead of jumping right in, slow down and pay careful to your conscience. In the end, you'll be very glad you did.

Your conscience is your alarm system. It's your protection.

CHARLES STANLEY

323
When Things Go Wrong

I do not consider myself yet to have taken hold of it. But one thing I do: Forgetting what is behind and straining toward what is ahead, I press on toward the goal to win the prize for which God has called me heavenward in Christ Jesus.

PHILIPPIANS 3:13–14 NIV

When things go wrong, you can always talk to your parents, and you can always talk to God.

Your parents love you, and they always want to know what you're worried about. And the very same God who created the universe stands ready and willing to comfort you, too. So, when things go haywire, talk to your parents and pray about the things that concern you. When you do, you'll feel better because you'll know that you're never alone and that you don't have to solve your problems by yourself.

A Timely Tip

When things go wrong, it's easy to become discouraged. But a far better plan is this: work hard to change the things you can change, and pray about the things you can't change.

324
Obey God and Be Happy

*I will praise you, LORD, with all my heart. I will tell all
the miracles you have done. I will be happy because of you;
God Most High, I will sing praises to your name.*

PSALM 9:1–2 NCV

Do you want to be happy? Then follow your conscience
and make sure that your actions agree with your beliefs.
Why? Because if you believe one thing but do something
else, your conscience simply won't allow you to enjoy the
good feelings that can—and should—be yours.

So today, be sure that you obey God's Word and listen
to the conscience that He has placed in your heart. When
you do, the Lord will honor your good works, and your
good works will honor Him. And everybody will be happy.

* * *

*If our hearts have been attuned to God
through an abiding faith in Christ,
the result will be joyous optimism and good cheer.*

BILLY GRAHAM

✳ ✳ ✳
325
He Is Here

Every morning he wakes me. He teaches me to listen
like a student. The Lord GOD helps me learn.

ISAIAH 50:4–5 NCV

Wherever you happen to be, God is there, too. If you're at home, the Lord is there. If you're at school or a church, He's there, too. It's good to know that your Father in heaven is everywhere you've ever been and everyplace you'll ever go. That means that you can talk to Him whenever you like.

God doesn't take vacations, and He doesn't play hide-and-seek. He's always "right here, right now," waiting to hear from you. So if you're wondering where God is, wonder no more. He's here. And that's a promise!

☞ Remember This

God isn't very far away. In fact, wherever you happen to be, He's there too. So you can always say a prayer, and He'll always hear you.

326
Just Try Your Best

Whatever you do, work at it with all your heart,
as working for the Lord, not for men.

COLOSSIANS 3:23 NIV

God doesn't expect you to be perfect, but He does want you to try hard. And He wants you to be cheerful and enthusiastic about your work.

When you do your best—at home, at church, at school, or anywhere else, for that matter—you'll feel better about yourself and you'll get more done. So try hard and don't worry if you make a few mistakes along the way. Nobody's perfect, but plenty of people work hard and do good things for God...and you can be one of those people.

 **A Timely Tip**

Don't worry too much about the things you can't control. Just do your best and leave the rest up to God.

*** * ***

327
It's Better to Give

In every way I've shown you that by laboring like this,
it is necessary to help the weak and to keep in mind
the words of the Lord Jesus, for He said,
"It is more blessed to give than to receive."

ACTS 20:35 HCSB

Jesus said that it's better to give than to receive. That means we should be generous with other people—but sometimes we don't feel much like sharing. Sometimes it's so much easier to receive than give!

The Lord wants each of us to be humble, cheerful givers. He knows how richly He's blessed us, and He wants us to share those blessings today, not tomorrow.

So the next time you see somebody who needs a helping hand, a kind word, a pat on the back, or just about anything else for that matter, do the right thing: share. When you do, you'll make everybody a little happier, and you'll make God happy, too.

*** * ***

It is the duty of every Christian to be Christ to his neighbor.

MARTIN LUTHER

✳ ✳ ✳

328
God Will Forgive You

The Lord is merciful and compassionate,
slow to get angry and filled with unfailing love.
The Lord is good to everyone.
He showers compassion on all his creation.

PSALM 145:8–9 NLT

Even if you're a very good person, you're bound to make mistakes. After all, nobody's perfect.

When you make a mistake, you must try your best to learn from it. And if you have hurt someone or if you have disobeyed God, you must ask Him for forgiveness.

When you ask the Lord to forgive you, He will always do it. So, if you've made a mistake, tell God you're sorry. And then be sure that you don't make that same mistake again.

☞ Remember This

You cannot do anything that God can't forgive. God stands ready to forgive. All you have to do is ask.

✳ ✳ ✳

329
Be Kind to People in Need

Whatever you did for one of the least
of these brothers of Mine, you did for Me.

MATTHEW 25:40 HCSB

Jesus said that whenever we help people in need, we're helping Him, too. And since we owe everything to our Savior, that means we should always be kind and helpful to folks who can't help themselves.

Talk to your parents about ways you can share your blessings. Jesus wants you to be generous, especially to those who need your help the most.

✳ ✳ ✳

When you extend hospitality to others, you're not trying
to impress people, you're trying to reflect God to them.

MAX LUCADO

✳︎ ✳︎ ✳︎

330
Learn to Put First Things First

Happy is the person who finds wisdom,
the one who gets understanding.

PROVERBS 3:13 NCV

What's the most important thing you'll do today? Go to school? Do your homework? Play with your friends? These things may seem important to you, but they're certainly not the most important things on your to-do list. The most important thing you'll do today is to put God first by following in the footsteps of His Son.

In the life of every Christian, God should come first. That means He should come first in your life, too. So today and every day, put first things first by starting the day and finishing the day with God. Obey Him; trust Him; talk to Him; and welcome His Son into your heart.

✳︎ ✳︎ ✳︎

Jesus Christ is the first and last, author and finisher,
beginning and end, alpha and omega, and by Him
all other things hold together. He must be first
or nothing. God never comes next!

VANCE HAVNER

✳ ✳ ✳

331
Be Obedient to God

But Peter and the apostles replied,
"We must obey God rather than men."

ACTS 5:29 HCSB

God loves you, and He wants you to love Him. So how can you show God how much love and gratitude you have in your heart? By obeying His commandments, that's how. When you follow God's rules, you show Him the respect that He deserves.

Good things happen when you obey the Lord. And the sooner you learn to obey, the sooner those good things will start happening *to you*.

✳ ✳ ✳

Obedience is the outward expression of your love of God.

HENRY BLACKABY

* * *

332
Your Problems =
God's Opportunities

God's way is perfect. All the LORD's promises prove true.
He is a shield for all who look to him for protection.

PSALM 18:30 NLT

When things go wrong, what do you do? Do you pout, or whine, or give up? Hopefully not, because there's a better way. When you have a problem, you should pray about it, you should talk to your parents about it, and you should try to fix it, if you can. And you should pray about it, too.

Hidden beneath every problem is the seed of a solution— God's solution. Your job is to trust the Lord and look for His solutions, the ones that are right for you.

Your problems may seem too big to fix. But when God looks at them, He's not worried. The Lord can do anything, which means He can solve any problem, including yours.

* * *

Every problem is a character-building opportunity,
and the more difficult it is, the greater the potential
for building spiritual muscle.

RICK WARREN

333
Nobody's Perfect

*If we confess our sins to him, he is faithful and just
to forgive us our sins and to cleanse us from.*

1 JOHN 1:9 NLT

Nobody's perfect, not even you! Even if you're a very good person, even if you try hard to obey God's rules, you're bound to make mistakes. Everybody does.

When you make a mistake, you should try to learn from it (so that you won't make the same mistake again). And, if you've hurt someone—or if you've disobeyed God—you should ask for forgiveness.

When you ask for His forgiveness, God will forgive and forget. He doesn't expect you to be perfect. He loves you, imperfections and all.

 **A Timely Tip**

God knows you're not perfect, and He loves you anyway. So, if you make a mistake, don't be too hard on yourself. Nobody's perfect, and you shouldn't expect to be perfect, either.

✳ ✳ ✳

334

Be Generous Now

Each of you should give as you have decided in your heart to give.
You should not be sad when you give, and you should not give because
you feel forced to give. God loves the person who gives happily.

2 CORINTHIANS 9:7 NCV

You've probably heard it many times from your parents and teachers: "Share your things!" But it's important to realize that sharing isn't just something that grown-ups want you to do. It's also something that God wants you to do.

The word "possessions" is another way of describing the stuff that belongs to you: your clothes, your toys, your books, and the other things you own. Jesus said that you should learn how to share your possessions without feeling bad about it. Sometimes, of course, it's hard to be generous and easy to be stingy. But God wants you to be a cheerful giver today and every day. And since that's what God wants, it's what you should want, too.

✳ ✳ ✳

It's not difficult to make an impact on your world. All you
really have to do is put the needs of others ahead of your own.
You can make a difference with a little time and a big heart.

JAMES DOBSON

* * *
335
Think Ahead

Careful planning puts you ahead in the long run;
hurry and scurry puts you further behind.

PROVERBS 21:5 MSG

The Bible teaches us that it's good to think ahead and plan ahead. But sometimes, especially when we're in a hurry, it's just easier to act first and think about the consequences later.

If you're one of those boys who does things in a hurry, maybe it's time for a change. Maybe it's time to slow down and think things through before you take a big step, not after.

Your life is a series of choices. God wants you to choose wisely. Usually, you make the best decisions when you plan ahead. If you want to lead a life that is pleasing to God, you must make choices that are pleasing to Him. He deserves no less…and neither, for that matter, do you.

 **A Timely Tip**

It's easy to act without thinking, but acting too quickly can sometimes cause big problems. So slow yourself down and think before you act. It's the smart way to live.

***

336
The Best Excuse Is No Excuse

Each will be rewarded for his own work.

1 CORINTHIANS 3:8 NCV

It's easy to make up an excuse. People do it all the time. They simply invent "believable" reasons why they didn't do what they should have done in the first place. Then they blame somebody, or something, for their problems.

Please don't get into the habit of making excuses. Why? Because excuses don't work. And why don't they work? Simple. Since so many people have already made up so many excuses, we've heard them all before. The really "good" excuses have been used so many times that nobody believes them anymore.

So the next time you're tempted to make up an excuse, don't do it. Instead of explaining why you didn't do the work, do the work. After all, the very best excuse...is no excuse.

***

Replace your excuses with fresh determination.

CHARLES SWINDOLL

* * *
337
If You're Trying to Be Perfect

If you wait for perfect conditions,
you will never get anything done.

ECCLESIASTES 11:4 NLT

If you're trying to be perfect, you're going to be disappointed. Nobody's perfect, including you.

In the game of life, God expects you to try, but He doesn't always expect you to win. Sometimes you'll make mistakes, and that's okay with Him. The Lord understands, and He's quick to forgive.

So remember this: You don't have to be perfect to be a wonderful person. In fact, you don't even need to be "almost-perfect." You simply must try your best and leave the rest up to God.

* * *

What makes a Christian a Christian
is not perfection but forgiveness.

MAX LUCADO

338
Get Enough Rest

I said to myself, "Relax and rest.
God has showered you with blessings."

PSALM 116:7 MSG

If you're like most kids, you probably need nine or ten hours of sleep each night. But you may be trying to get by on less sleep than that. Why? Because you have so many screens, and there are so many interesting things to watch.

The next time you're tempted to stay up past your bedtime, don't beg your parents for "just a few more minutes" of screen time. Instead, remember that God wants you to get enough rest. And your parents want you to get enough rest. And your teachers want you to get enough sleep. And that's what you should want, too.

 A Timely Tip

To feel your best and do your best, you probably need nine to twelve hours of sleep each night. So be sure you go to bed early enough to get the sleep you need.

✳ ✳ ✳

339

Try to Please God with Your Thoughts and Prayers

May the words of my mouth and the meditation of my heart
be pleasing to you, O LORD, my rock and my redeemer.

PSALM 19:14 NLT

Thoughts are powerful things. If you think good thoughts, you'll feel better about yourself, and you'll please God. But if you fall into the habit of thinking bad thoughts, you're heading for trouble, and fast.

Do you try to think good thoughts about your friends, your family, and yourself? Do you lift your hopes and prayers to God? Do you say no to people who want you to do bad things or think bad thoughts? The Bible says that you should.

The Bible teaches us to guard our thoughts against things that are hurtful or wrong. So remember this: when you turn away from bad thoughts and focus, instead, on God and His Son, you'll be protected, and you'll be blessed.

☞ Remember This

Prayer is a habit. Worship is a habit. Kindness is a habit. And if you want to please God, you'd better make sure that these habits are your habits.

340
Believe!

Be not afraid, only believe.

MARK 5:36 KJV

The Bible is God's gift to you. When you read it and believe it, you're showing God that you're grateful for His gift.

God has made many promises to you, and you can be sure that He's going to keep every single one of them. When you believe in the Lord and trust Him, you have nothing to fear. Why? Because God will protect you now and forever. It's a promise you can depend on.

✳ ✳ ✳

It takes faith to obey God,
but God always rewards obedient faith.

WARREN WIERSBE

341
Sharing the Good News

Go therefore and make disciples of all the nations, baptizing them
in the name of the Father and of the Son and of the Holy Spirit,
teaching them to observe all things that I have commanded you;
and lo, I am with you always, even to the end of the age.

MATTHEW 28:19–20 NKJV

As Christians, all of us should be sharing God's Good News with people in our neighborhoods and people all over the world. But sometimes we're too shy or too afraid to talk about Jesus. So we keep our beliefs and our feelings to ourselves.

When it comes to our faith, God doesn't want us to stay silent. He wants us to talk about His Son.

Jesus commands us to become "fishers of men." And, the time to go fishing is now. So don't keep your faith to yourself. Tell people what Christ means to you. They need to hear it, and you need to say it. So don't delay; start talking about Jesus today…and never stop.

☞ Remember This

If you're willing, God will use you to share His message. If you're willing to share the Good News, God will guide you and bless you.

* * *

342
Take the Right Path

*Trust in the LORD with all your heart; do not depend
on your own understanding. Seek his will in all you do,
and he will show you which path to take.*

PROVERBS 3:5–6 NLT

The Bible promises that God has a plan for you. If you obey Him and trust Him, He will guide you along the best path for you. So here's what you should do: Read His Word every day, pray often, and, most importantly, welcome Jesus into your heart. When you do these things, God will bless you and guide you, now and forever.

God wants you to keep learning. And He wants you to keep growing in your faith. So let the Lord lead the way. Your job is to trust, to obey, and to follow wherever He leads.

* * *

*When it comes to walking with God,
there is no such thing as instant maturity.
God doesn't mass produce His saints. He hand tools each one.*

CHARLES SWINDOLL

343
Don't Play the Blame Game

People's own foolishness ruins their lives,
but in their minds they blame the LORD.

PROVERBS 19:3 NCV

If something goes wrong, it's easy to look for somebody—anybody—to blame. But God doesn't want you to play the blame game. He wants you to admit your mistakes and learn from them. And you should want the very same thing.

Everybody makes mistakes, but not everybody learns from them. The people who try to pretend they're perfect may blame other people, or they even blame God for their troubles! But you should be smarter than that. You should realize that God doesn't expect you to be perfect, but He does want you to be honest with yourself, with your friends, and with your family. So the next time you encounter trouble, don't look for somebody to blame; look for a way to fix the problem. When you do, everybody wins.

✳ ✳ ✳

The main thing is this: we should never blame anyone or
anything for our defeats. No matter how evil their intentions
may be, they are altogether unable to harm us until we begin
to blame them and use them as excuses for our own unbelief.

A. W. TOZER

＊＊＊

344
Be Happy

Happy are the people who live at your Temple....
Happy are those whose strength comes from you.

PSALM 84:4–5 NCV

If you're looking for something to be happy about, you won't have to look very far. After all, God has given you more blessings than you can count, and He's promised that you can live with Him, forever, in heaven.

Happiness goes hand in hand with good behavior. The happiest people do not misbehave; the happiest people are not mean or stingy. The happiest people don't say unkind things. The happiest people are those who love the Lord and follow His rules—starting, of course, with the Golden one.

So, if you want to be *really* happy, be grateful for your blessings and obey God. When you do, you'll never stay sad for long.

＊＊＊

Happiness is obedience, and obedience is happiness.

C. H. SPURGEON

*** * *

345
Make Choices That Are Pleasing to God

LORD, teach me your demands,
and I will keep them until the end.

PSALM 119:33 NCV

Every day you make lots of choices. From the moment you wake up in the morning until the time you nod off to sleep at night, you make all sorts of decisions: decisions about the things you do, decisions about the things you say, and decisions about the thoughts you choose to think.

If you want to lead a life that is pleasing to God, your choices must be pleasing to Him. When you please God you'll be blessed because of your obedience. So don't delay; make wise choices today and every day.

* * *

Sin always robs us; obedience always enriches us.

WARREN WIERSBE

346
Miracles Great and Small

For nothing will be impossible with God.

Luke 1:37 HCSB

Is anything impossible for God? Nope. He can do anything. No miracles are too hard for Him.

The Lord does amazing things in amazing ways, and if you pay attention, you might even see Him doing wonderful with your own two eyes. So don't try to put limits on God. His miracles come in all shapes and sizes, so keep your eyes and your heart open. Be watchful, and you'll soon be amazed.

✳ ✳ ✳

When God is involved, anything can happen.

Charles Swindoll

347
The One Hundredth Psalm

one hundredth psalm is about being grateful.
You can memorize it if you try:

*Make a joyful shout to the L*ORD*, all you lands!*
*Serve the L*ORD *with gladness;*
Come before His presence with singing.
*Know that the L*ORD*, He is God;*
It is He who has made us, and not we ourselves;
We are His people and the sheep of His pasture.

Enter into His gates with thanksgiving,
And into His courts with praise.
Be thankful to Him, and bless His name.
*For the L*ORD *is good;*
His mercy is everlasting,
And His truth endures to all generations. (NKJV)

✳ ✳ ✳

348
It's Good to Share

A generous person will be enriched.

Proverbs 11:25 HCSB

The Bible teaches us that it's good to share. The Lord wants us to be helpful, cheerful, kind, and generous. And when we're generous, He gives us more blessings than we can count.

When you're trying to make a list of the things you can share, you probably begin by looking at the things that belong to you (like toys or clothes), but there are many more things you can share (like love, kindness, encouragement, and prayers). That means you have the opportunity to share something with somebody almost any time you want. And that's exactly what God wants you to do—so start sharing now and don't ever stop.

☞ Remember This

God gave you blessings so you can use them and share them. Today is the right day to use your talents and share your blessings.

✳ ✳ ✳

349

It Pays to Have a Good Attitude

Make me hear joy and gladness.

PSALM 51:8 NKJV

It pays to have a good attitude. So, where does a good attitude begin? It starts in our hearts and works its way out from there. It's up to each of us to fill our hearts with love for God, love for Jesus, and love for all people. When we do, good things happen.

Sometimes, of course, we don't feel like celebrating. Sometimes, when we're angry, or frustrated, or tired, we may whine, and pout, and do little else. On those days when we're feeling bad, we should try to calm down and rest up.

Do you want to be the best person you can be? Then you shouldn't grow tired of doing the right things, and you shouldn't ever grow tired of thinking the right thoughts.

✳ ✳ ✳

Often, attitude is the only difference between success and failure.

JOHN MAXWELL

***
350
Be Kind and Humble

Now finally, all of you should be like-minded and sympathetic,
should love believers, and be compassionate and humble.

1 PETER 3:8 HCSB

God wants you to be kind and humble. He wants you to say kind things, and He wants you to do good deeds. But He doesn't want you to brag about all the fine things you've done. It's not enough to be helpful; God also wants you to be modest.

When you stop to think about it, it doesn't really make sense to be filled with pride. After all, everything we have is a gift from the Lord, so He deserves the praise, not us. So the next time you're tempted to brag about something you did, remind yourself that God is the One who really deserves the credit. Then do the right thing: praise Him, not yourself.

☞ Remember This

When you're humble and kind, people will notice. And so will God. He rewards kind people—like you—who try hard to follow in the footsteps of His Son.

351
Don't Be Too Quick to Judge

Do not judge others, and you will not be judged.
Do not condemn others, or it will all come back against you.
Forgive others, and you will be forgiven.

LUKE 6:37 NLT

The Bible teaches us that we shouldn't judge other people. In fact, God's Word warns us that if we judge others too harshly, God will judge us in the same way.

The Bible also promises that if we forgive other people, we will be forgiven, too. What does it all mean? It means that the Lord wants to forgive other people without judging them.

Are you tempted to blame people, criticize people, or judge people? If so, remember this: God is already judging what people do, and He doesn't need—or want—your help. So don't judge!

👉 Remember This

God doesn't want you to judge other people. He knows enough to judge them, but you don't. So, don't judge.

Wisdom from the Heart

Knowing what is right is like deep water in the heart;
a wise person draws from the well within.

PROVERBS 20:5 MSG

God gave you something called a conscience: it's that little feeling that tells you whether something is right or wrong. Your conscience will usually tell you what to do and when to do it. Trust that feeling.

If you stop to listen to your conscience, you'll make better decisions. Why? Because your conscience is a wise counselor that always leads you in the right direction. It's wisdom from the heart.

So if your conscience speaks, listen carefully. Listen *very* carefully.

 **A Timely Tip**

When your conscience speaks, listen carefully. Listening to your conscience is the smart way to live.

＊＊＊
353
Be Good to Your Parents

Honor your father and your mother.
EXODUS 20:12 HCSB

In the Ten Commandments, God instructs us to honor and respect our parents. So here's a question for you: are you the kind of boy who helps and respects his parents? Hopefully the answer is a great big yes. After all, your parents love you more than you can imagine, and they work very hard to take care of you. So it's no wonder that the Lord wants you to be kind and respectful.

Today and every day, give your parents the respect they deserve. You'll make them happy...and you'll make your heavenly Father happy, too.

☞ Remember This

God wants you to help and respect your parents. And if that's what God wants, you should want it, too.

* * *
354
Hopes, Hopes, and More Hopes

Now may the God of hope fill you with all joy
and peace in believing, so that you may overflow
with hope by the power of the Holy Spirit.

ROMANS 15:13 HCSB

*A*re you excited about your life, your school, your faith, and your future? You should be. After all, God is on your side, and if you have welcomed God's Son into your heart, then your future is intensely and eternally bright.

The Lord has a plan for your life that only He can see. Trust Him today and every day. He has promised to protect you now and forever. And with God as your protector, you can be sure that your life's story will have a very happy ending.

So don't be afraid to have high hopes and big dreams. Good things are in store for you, now and forever. It's a promise.

☞ Remember This

As a boy who loves Jesus, you have every reason to be hopeful about your future here on earth and your future in heaven. God is good, and you are safe.

✳ ✳ ✳

355
Trouble Doesn't Last Forever

People who do what is right may have many problems,
but the LORD will solve them all.

PSALM 34:19 NCV

Have you ever been disappointed by the way things turned out? Have you ever wanted something that you didn't get or had a dream that didn't come true? Probably so. But when you're disappointed or sad, please remember this: your troubles are temporary, but God's love lasts forever.

God is bigger than your problems, so there's no need to worry. Just trust the Lord, obey Him, and do your fair share of the work. When you've done your part, you can be sure that He will do His part. When He does, good things are bound to happen.

☞ Remember This

If you've got a problem, talk about it with your parents. It doesn't pay to keep everything bottled up inside.

356
Your Shining Light

You are the light of the world. A city situated on a hill cannot be hidden. No one lights a lamp and puts it under a basket, but rather on a lampstand, and it gives light for all who are in the house. In the same way, let your light shine before men, so that they may see your good works and give glory to your Father in heaven.

MATTHEW 5:14–16 HCSB

The Bible says that you are "the light of the world." The Bible also says that you should live in a way that lets other people understand what it means to be a good person and a good Christian.

What kind of "light" have you been giving off? Hopefully you have been a good example for everybody to see. Why? Because the world needs all the light it can get, and that includes your light, too!

* * *

More depends on my walk than my talk.

D. L. MOODY

*** ** ***

357
God's Perfect Love

This is what real love is: It is not our love for God;
it is God's love for us. He sent his Son
to die in our place to take away our sins.

1 JOHN 4:10 NCV

The Bible makes this amazing promise: God is love. It's a big promise, a very important description of what God is and how God adores His children.

God's love is perfect. When we open our hearts to Him—and when we let His Son rule over our lives—we are blessed and we are protected.

Today, offer sincere prayers of thanksgiving to your heavenly Father. When you accept God's grace and share the His love, you'll be blessed here on earth and throughout all eternity. Accept His perfect love today.

☞ Remember This

God's love for you is perfect. He loves you all the time, and He's with you every minute of the day. He's always ready to hear your prayers, so pray often and thank Him often.

* * *

358
Success According to God

*Live the way the LORD your God has commanded
you so that you may live and have what is good.*

DEUTERONOMY 5:33 NCV

What does success mean to you? Does it mean making lots of money, or owning lots of stuff? If so, you're on the wrong track. The Bible teaches us that real success has nothing to do with fame or fortune; it has everything to do with God's gift of love and His promise of eternal life.

If you have welcomed Jesus into your heart, you're already a huge success, but there is still more that you can do. You can tell people about Jesus, and you can show them what it means to be a faithful Christian. You can be kind, generous, honest, and faithful. And you can love the Lord with all your heart. When you do these things you will be successful in the eyes of God…and that's the only kind of success that really matters.

* * *

Bible history is filled with people who began the race with great success but failed at the end because they disregarded God's rules.

WARREN WIERSBE

359
When Friends Misbehave

Love from the center of who you are; don't fake it.
Run for dear life from evil; hold on for dear life to good.

ROMANS 12:9–10 MSG

Do your friends behave themselves? Are they kind to you and kind to other people, too? If so, congratulations! If not, it's probably time to start looking for a few new friends. After all, it's really not very much fun to be around people who constantly misbehave.

The Bible teaches that a pure heart is a wonderful blessing. It's up to each of us to fill our hearts with love for God, love for Jesus, and love for all people.

Do you want to be the best person you can be? Then invite the love of Christ into your heart and find friends who will do the same. You'll be glad you did, and your friends will be glad, too.

 A Timely Tip

Since you'll be tempted to behave like your friends, pick friends who behave themselves.

God Knows What He's Doing. Trust Him.

"I say this because I know what I am planning for you,"
says the LORD. "I have good plans for you, not plans
to hurt you. I will give you hope and a good future."

JEREMIAH 29:11 NCV

God is good, and He is in charge, even when bad things happen. Sometimes we can't figure out why the Lord does things. But even when we can't understand God's reasons, we can trust His promises.

God loves you, and He has promised to protect you in good times and hard times. So when unfortunate things happen, don't worry. The Lord is watching over you. And because you have welcomed Jesus into your heart, you're safe today, tomorrow, and forever.

＊ ＊ ＊

Mary could not have dreamed all that would result from
her faithful obedience. Likewise, you cannot possibly imagine
all that God has in store for you when you trust Him.

HENRY BLACKABY

✳ ✳ ✳

361

God Has Given You Gifts You Can Use

God has given each of you a gift from his great variety
of spiritual gifts. Use them well to serve one another.

1 PETER 4:10 NLT

In the whole universe, there's only one you. You're one-of-a-kind, a very special person with very special talents. Your particular talents are a gift from God, and He wants you to use them for His glory.

So here's a question: how will you use your talents today? God wants you to use them to become a better person and a better Christian. And He will help you make the most of the gifts He has given you. So pray for guidance and get busy. Today, like every other day, is a wonderful time to use your talents for the good of God's kingdom.

👉 Remember This

God has given you special gifts for a reason: to share them.

❋ ❋ ❋
362
God Will Help You

*God is working in you to help you want to do
and be able to do what pleases him.*

PHILIPPIANS 2:13 NCV

If you need help, there are plenty of people you can talk to, starting with your parents. You can also talk things over with teachers, grandparents, brothers, sisters, friends, and just about anybody else you trust. But there's another place you can go when you have a problem: you can go to the Lord.

God has promised to help you when you need it. So, don't be afraid to ask Him for the things you need. He's listening, and He wants to hear from you. Now.

☞ Remember This

When you ask God for help, He will give it. So if there's something you really need, pray about it. God is listening, and He wants to hear from you now.

✳ ✳ ✳

363
Guard Your Thoughts

Be careful what you think, because your thoughts run your life.

Proverbs 4:23 NCV

God wants you to think good thoughts; He wants you to be happy; and He wants you to behave yourself. To do these things, you need to guard your thoughts against anything that might tempt you to disobey Him.

The Lord has created a beautiful world, and there are many wonderful things to look at. But there are also many things that are scary, or hurtful, or harmful to your faith. So be careful what you watch and be careful what you think. Look for things that bring you closer to God, and avoid anything that might cause you to misbehave. Protect your mind and your heart today, tomorrow, and every day.

✳ ✳ ✳

If your mind is filled with the Word of God,
then it can't be filled with impure thoughts.

David Jeremiah

364
Finishing Your Work

It is better to finish something than to start it.
It is better to be patient than to be proud.

ECCLESIASTES 7:8 NCV

When you find yourself in the middle of a hard job, are you tempted to quit? If so, you're not alone. From time to time, everybody feels the temptation to give up. The next time you feel the urge to quit, remember this: Whatever your problem, God can handle it. Your job is to keep working until He does.

Jesus finished what He began, and so should you. Jesus didn't give in, and neither should you. Jesus did what was right, and so should you. So, when you have important work to do, don't be a quitter; be a finisher.

 A Timely Tip

Usually, getting started is easier than finishing. But the biggest rewards go to the people who finish the things they start. So, when you start something, finish it. You'll feel better when you do.

✳ ✳ ✳

365
Always Put God First

*Jesus answered, "'Love the Lord your God with all
your heart, all your soul, and all your mind.'
This is the first and most important command."*

MATTHEW 22:37–38 NCV

The Bible teaches us that we should always put God first in our lives. Yet all too often, we place our Lord in second, third, or fourth place while we worship other things. It's a mistake to put God in second place, but sometimes we do it anyway, and we create big problems for ourselves.

Does God rule your heart? Make certain that the honest answer to this question is yes. In the life of every Christian, God should come first. And that's precisely the place that He deserves in your heart.

☞ Remember This

God deserves first place in your heart, and you deserve the experience of putting Him there and keeping Him there.